My Aran Life In Me

Ronan Faherty

Ronan Faherty

This book is dedicated to all the care staff that took care of me through the years.

A special thank you to my good friend Connor – this dream would not be a reality without you.

A special thank you to my sister-in-law Kari for the formatting and publishing help.

Onaght
My home today

Oat Quarter
My Nana's home in 1980

Kilronan
Ferry boat dock

Inis Mor
Aran Islands

Chapter 1

"All our dreams can come true, if we have the courage to pursue them."

~ Walt Disney

My name is Ronan Faherty. I am an island man, and also, a disabled man. I once read that "to explore an island, one must risk obsession." That is certainly the case for all island lovers and could also be said about exploring one's self. Thinking about writing my own story, it is fair to say that I have gone dangerously close to risking obsession and have spent a lot of time looking at my life and thinking about the path my life has taken. This has been more than just self-indulgence or self-obsession. I have thought long and hard about whether the story of my life is worth telling and whether I am right or wrong, I would very much like to tell my own story.

I had a road accident back in 1980 at the age of 5, and the consequences for all concerned have been both life-changing and challenging. I would like to state in the strongest terms possible, that the accident was just that – it was an unfortunate accident that has been difficult at times, but it was a genuine accident.

I live on Inis Mor, the largest of the Aran Islands, off the west coast of Ireland, near both sides of my family. For generations, many people, both indigenes and visitors have written wonderful things about my home island. Some of these people are related to me and I must confess, I love every of these writings as they have been a major source of inspiration. My story diverges from these writings in that I identify with the love of this impossibly beautiful island and I can honestly and proudly say that it means as much to me as to any of them, but there is a difference. The difference is that I share their views, and in many cases, their experiences – but, my unique viewpoint is from two perspectives. The first being that I am an island man and the other being that I am disabled.

I have thought very carefully about both, and truth be told, if I were to focus exclusively on one over the other, I would not be telling my own story. One of the daily challenges I face is to live in the world first and foremost as a man but not ignoring the fact that due to a childhood accident, I am disabled. My daily challenge then is not to allow my disability to define me. This challenge is primarily one that I try to deal with and accept internally as I have believed for all my life that it is essentially an inside job.

Being limited in my mobility and consequently, having my life choices restricted has given me the blessing of thinking carefully and deeply about the world and my place in it. Like every journey, it starts with a single step. My internal journey has encompassed the whole gamut of human emotions which are joys and fears. My life today is like everyone else's on the surface of the earth and for sure, I have feelings, dreams and fears like anyone else. I think it is fair enough to let you know that I do not in any way feel sorry for myself and as I describe my life, I need you to just see it as nothing but an honest description. When I wake up in the morning, instead of jumping out of my bed to face the day, I have a physical challenge of getting out of bed and then getting dressed. Again, my motivation is to attempt to give the best and most honest description of my life that I can. There is a difference in the start to my day compared to others, but I eventually discovered a truism: comparisons are odious!

Although, I would honestly prefer to be able to jump out of bed and hit the ground running, the fact that I can't is no longer an obstacle or a barrier to me. I am finally in a place of semi-comfortable acceptance that while my life may be different, it is not necessarily worse. As I sit here by my keyboard at the western end of this Island, typing away, I am very conscious of the fact that in giving a fair and honest description of my day to day challenges, it may feel like a report of some sort to you readers.   The area that challenges me a bit and the area that I find hard to articulate is the subject matter that I actually need to write, and that is how the consequences of my childhood accident had impact on me internally.

I would love to state that acceptance is a happy place that you attain and then dwell in, but as most human beings will attest, that is not the case. I find that almost every single day, I find myself feeling negative and lacking acceptance around my life as it is. These feelings are black and terrible as they make me feel such unwelcome feelings like anger, resentment and bitterness. Dealing with my brain injury hurts emotionally and it visits me on an almost daily basis. I am not 100% sure what specifically triggers these thoughts and feelings but generally they seem to kick off from my own internal thoughts.

Now, I know from the pattern of my life that I cannot mentally and emotionally afford to let this blackness and negativity rule my life. So, over the years, just as I have become accustomed to having a daily visit from negatives, I have now become somewhat skilled at counteracting these imposters. My reality is that the process of countering the negativity varies from day to day but a common theme and practice for me is counting my blessings and trying to show gratitude. It is a process that varies in its intensity from day to day and the way out each day requires different level of emotional strength. I honestly feel that my family, my mother in particular, has given me the tools needed to battle on a daily basis.

When I am struggling to cope with the way my life is, I often find myself dealing with a deep kind of anger. Now, I am very aware that logically there are reasonable answers to everything but there is a period almost every day that the distance between what is logical and my emotions seems very vast and one that at that any given time I feel like I can't bridge. However, my life experience has shown me that once I stick to it and persevere, my emotions and feelings will eventually catch up with my reality and then I would be able to cope for another day and I am pleased to say that I usually access that elusive animal called acceptance. There are many opportunities for me in writing this book, which is essentially my own life story. One opportunity is simply in telling my story, but it is also exciting for me that perhaps the telling of my story might motivate or help others.

I am 41 years of age and I live in Inis Mor with my mother Agnes. As I live and work on my home island, I am aware and very understanding and indeed forgiving about how people sometimes view me. I completely understand that it is a part of human nature to want things and people to be wrapped up neatly and placed in boxes.

While I understand and get this – one of my challenges has been not to lazily flop into one of those ready-made boxes that others have created. I can't be sure where the burning desire to live my life to the fullest and to be true to myself came from. There is something in the psyche of all island people in that our ancestors chose to buck the trends and conventional wisdom of the time and chose to live on an island. It takes a form of pioneering spirit, independence and confidence to choose this island as a place to live. I also think that hidden, not so carefully in the island people, is a rebelliousness of some sort. I love all these qualities and while I am genuinely not 100% sure if this may or may not be in my DNA, I have found a way of accessing these qualities that has facilitated my recovery – mainly by having the burning desire not to lie down, limit myself and most of all, my point blank refusal to be defined or boxed in by anything.

I would like to give a very human, honest and realistic account of my accident, treatment, recovery and my associated feelings in hopes to share my world with you all. I am reminded, before I share the next piece, of a chance meeting that I had with a neighbour of mine from the Western end of this island, Martín Choilin Tom (Mullin) – and during our conversation, he said to me, "Everyone has a disability, it's just that it's more visible in some than others".

I took this seriously as he has a disability himself; he has only one leg and whether he did or not, I found this statement to be fascinating, refreshing and liberating. I sometimes can get caught in a cycle of thoughts where I feel that I am the only one in the world with a disability. Now, I know that this is not true. I can readily accept my situation and can also express gratitude for my life, which very often is the key to unlocking a negative thought cycle. On a bad day, I can usually break out of the negative thought cycle, but it just takes longer and is more painful. It has happened on more occasions than I could relay that people have said stuff to me that has initially helped me beyond measure but more importantly, very often, these same freely given gems of wisdom have gone on to become part of my life skills and coping mechanisms for living with my own disability on a daily basis.

I am neither trying to diminish my daily challenges nor am I attempting to seek any different treatment, my hope is that, like everyone else, I have exactly the same feelings, but my wish is that I can somehow articulate my own unique journey as an island Man, who happens to also be disabled. In writing this story of my life, there is one possible outcome that both excites and motivates me and that is that I may be able to help someone else in the telling of my own life story. Other people have encountered and conquered greater obstacles, but my own story is the only one that

I can tell, and I pray that I do my family, friends, community and myself justice. It may appear to others that I am in a form of prison in my body but please know that I am not.

One thing that I discovered some years ago is that I like writing poems. I started writing them when I was in school and have drawn a huge amount of satisfaction, comfort and enjoyment in writing these personal and humble poems. I would like to put a few of them into this book as they mean a lot to me, and in some ways, they reflect and express my values and thoughts better than anything.

I still enjoy writing and have been writing a Facebook blog for 2 years now, which mainly consists of my own thoughts and feelings along with sharing my day to day experiences of my life on the island --- I usually finish off each week with a quote of my own or from someone else, the one below is my own.

"People with physical and mental disabilities deserve a better life."
~Ronan Faherty

Even though my memories are not great about the chronology and specifics of my childhood, it is more than clear to me that I had a strong set of internal feelings and priorities that, like today, were hard to articulate, but please know that my feelings, fears and dreams are the very same for me as for anyone else. Sometimes a child's feelings can be dismissed or even trivialized. Sometimes as a grown man, I experience this same inadvertent and careless dismissal of my feelings today. Even though I know in my heart, that people do not mean to be offensive, but the set of feelings, values and fears that I had then are the same as today. I am very understanding and compassionate about how people only mean well, but the form of internal prison that I had after my childhood accident has become a feature of my everyday life since then. I may struggle at times to express myself to the satisfaction of others, but please know that my feelings are as real and valid as anyone else.

The first poem that I ever wrote was called, Fishermen of the Deep. This poem is dedicated to fisherman all over the world. Please allow me to share it with you.

FISHERMEN OF THE DEEP

My father is a fisherman,
To sea he goes from day to night,
he catches fish of all sort and brings them home on ice.

The trawler rolls from side to side
with waves so high they reach the sky,
alone he stands in face of storm and breakfast in the cabin.

Miles to sea they go with wife and child left at home,
trawler full of silver blue they sense the storm they know it's due,
they dash for home to harbour wall where the anxious still wait's,
praying for all.

By Ronan Faherty

Chapter 2

"When one door closes, another opens;
but we often look so long and so regretfully upon the closed door that we do not
see the one which has opened for us."
~ Alexander Graham Bell

My life changed forever when I had an accident in the summer of 1980, at the age of 5. I can only remember my time before that as being a very happy lucky little boy whose only thoughts and feelings were pretty much the same as any other little boy's. I certainly never thought about my health or how great it was to be able to run, walk and jump at will. I am happy to have enjoyed the luxury of all these things and much more without knowing it or realizing it at all, I was in an enchanted and innocent happy state. All this soon changed for both myself and my family on that summer's day. I ran across the road near my house, as thousands of children have before, and a car came down the hill with what turned out to be cruel and merciless timing. I was hit. And in that moment, the path and direction of my life changed forever.

Before I attempt to write about the events and drama of the accident and life thereafter, I would like to say that I am finally at a place in my life that has made me realize that everyone in life has issues to deal with, and I can remember reading once "it's not what happens that defines you, it's what you do with it". I truthfully got dealt a tough hand to play and while I am certainly no saint, I have had the opportunity to grow by looking into my own soul every day, searching for strength and meaning. Most days I do okay, but some days I honestly feel I can't go on. My life's experience has clearly shown me that once I stick to it and don't give up, the sun always rises, and I always seem to find both acceptance and strength to keep on keeping on.

My life before my accident is a sort of a happy blur to me but one stand-out memory for me is the strong bond and relationship that I had back then with my brother, Rory. I am more than a small bit pleased to say that to this very day, we still enjoy that close bond and wonderful relationship. I cannot remember being in full health, and probably like most healthy people, I probably took it for granted. I am sure as a young child, I never considered anything but good health – what a lovely, happy memory and feeling. Casting my eyes back to those early days, I can clearly remember pushing Rory's bicycle up the hill to Fearann na Choirce National School – there were two main reasons for this which were built upon the fact that I idolized and loved my brother Rory, and wanted to show him in the only way that I knew how at the time, by bringing his bicycle up to him at the school so he could cycle home. I wouldn't be stretching it by saying that he was my hero.

The other reason for going up to Fearann na Choirce National School was that my mother's mother, my Mamo, Mairin Concannon, taught in that school and even though she gave so many children the gift of learning, my memory is more personal. I used to generally go up there at lunch time and would sit beside her at her big teacher's table and we would share lunch. I am probably being a bit economical with the truth when I say that we used to "share" lunch. The reality is that I would hungrily gobble down the entire lunch. It's like being a child and not having the awareness to appreciate and value good health.

One of the consequences of me eating my Mamo's lunch was that she was quietly hungry but she was secure in the knowledge that she would be calling unto my mother, Agnes on her way back home for her dinner and like a lot of households at that time, words and displays of love were scarce. But, as someone said to me years ago from that era "if love was bacon and cabbage, we got plenty ". The importance to both my mother and Mamo of these visits was much more than food, and the gentleness and respectful nature of these important visits is not lost on me today. In many ways, these kinds of actions and interactions were all along laying down and building the blocks for what would eventually evolve into my own value system and moral compass. To be honest, they are golden and priceless memories.

On my way to the school with Rory's bicycle I would also call unto my Father's Mother – Nonie Faherty – as she lived across the road from the school. Even though Nonie was a robust and forthright person, she reserved a special tenderness for her grandchildren, and in particular for me, which again was a treasured and priceless memory. Another small but insightful footnote to that memory was when my big brother Rory made his First Holy Communion in 1986. He was given a few pounds and rather than just spending it on himself, which would have been fine, he bought me a 3 wheeled bicycle out of his windfall. A gesture and action that means as much to me today as it did then, and I can truly say that kind action is the mark of the man.

1984, age 9 on my three-wheeled bicycle

Going back to that fateful day in 1980 that was to prove a turning point and defining moment in my life and that of my family's too. The medical side of my story is vital, but interspersed within my medical story are my own experiences and feelings – sometimes, stuff that was not strictly speaking explicable from a medical point of view occurred and with every twist and turn in my life, I am searching for the courage and inspiration to be open in the telling of my life story.

The images in my mind of a small dark haired boy lying on the tarmac road on Inis Mor, with blood coming out of his ears, are painful images for any human being to have in their mind and even if I live to be 100, I don't think that I'll ever be able to understand the sheer terror and instinctive feelings that my parents felt at that time. I know that they would gladly have laid down their own lives for their injured little boy. Thankfully, they didn't have to. I am not a parent so I can't write with 100%

confidence about those feelings that seem to be exclusive to parents but, it certainly is not lost on me as to the depth of feelings – good and bad – love and terror side by side, that they were experiencing at that time.

As mentioned, I innocently ran across the road and was hit by an oncoming car. My memories are completely blank from then as I was knocked unconscious. I usually rely on my mother, Agnes' memories which are as clear and painful to her today as was on that day. The sports were on in Kilronan that day and for various reasons there was no Doctor or Guard on the island. As I laid on the road, no one knew whether I was alive or dead. A tourist, a nurse, who was passing by on a jaunting cart stumbled upon my accident scene. In life, there is very often no explaining why things happen, be they good or bad, but this nurse stumbled upon my accident scene at a critical and important moment and she was able to give help and guidance which was to be vital.

I was transported by car to the small airport on the island and was brought to the plane and flown out to Galway where there was an ambulance and medical help waiting. Likely hours passed from the time of the accident until I was in the hands of medical professionals. All of this was organized and put in place primarily by my parents and if I live to be 100 years old, I doubt that I'll ever be able to understand fully the range of emotions and fears that they felt on that day and since. After the accident my parents' main and only real concern at that time was whether I would live.

Simultaneous to me being medivacked off my island home by plane, my parents had to get a boat to Rossaveal, which is a 45-minute journey, and then drive nearly an hour to Galway Regional Hospital, still not knowing if their little dark-haired boy was alive or dead. That is a journey that I can honestly only guess or surmise about, but I believe anyone, parent or not, could feel the anguish, fear and urgency on my parent's behalf. It is also not a minor

13

point that my mother was pregnant at that time, carrying my brother Donal.

Days later, I was transferred by ambulance to Richmond hospital in Dublin and there was in a coma for one month. And this is where the medical story and my human tale diverged for a short but deeply meaningful time. My father had gone back out to sea in an effort to support his family and keep up the repayments on his boat at the time – The Albatross. My mother was with me the whole time and my Mamo from the island was sending me tapes of my childhood friends playing and chatting, and my mother was talking to me nonstop to stimulate and hopefully waken me. One Saturday my older brother Rory was taken to Galway from the island, so my mother could go down and see her boy. In any event, my mother, as she always did, told me what she was doing, and even though I have no memory of it and the medics have no explanation for it – when my mother told me in my comatose state that she was going to Galway to visit my brother Rory, apparently, I woke and screamed for a brief moment.

My life and recovery, to date, has been sprinkled with inexplicable events, kind events and love – none of which make it on to my medical reports and records, but all have impacted my life in a way that has breathed life in to me and in many ways, made me who I am. In the month that followed in Dublin, slowly but surely, they saw signs of life in me as my eyes were flickering and other little movements occurred. The doctors then decided that I should be moved to Galway for the next part of my treatment and recovery. I started to make slow progress and very significantly, with hours and hours of medical help and familial love, I spoke my first word. My first word spoken was the word 'Mommy". I feel that the reaction I had in relation to hearing about my brother Rory and the fact that my first word was "mommy", is a huge insight as to how my tender and innocent

14

feelings were true and honest in the way I could express the depths of my heart and soul in the only way that I knew how.

The events of that day have affected my life and to a large extent, my family's lives. As a man, one of my greatest challenges has been to play this hand I've been given, and not allow self-pity or anger to fester which I feel I have managed to do with help from those who love me and care about me.

My story of treatment, recovery and island life is the only story I have and is my life. I will attempt to share it as honestly, openly and thoughtfully as I possibly can and even though it's a deeply personal journey, I hope that you will come with me.

Chapter 3

"Life's greatest happiness is to be convinced we are loved."

~ Victor Hugo

The heartbeat of my home island is community and the essence of community is family. Both sides of my family are islanders – and one of the unique characteristics of this is that I can see the traits, strengths, weaknesses that have come down through my family for generations. This visibility is like a double-edged sword, it is comforting, and it gives me a sense of belonging to be able to openly and visibly view the characteristics of my fore bearers but alongside that same comfort, lies the challenge of knowing about my people's nature but still forging ahead and being myself.

I feel it is important to my story that I give a brief background of my family and it would be only fair to say that their impact and influence on my life is immeasurable. I like to believe that for better or worse, I have become my own man, but I would not be painting the full picture if I were to leave out or gloss over the people who have gone before me.

I am aware that the following sentence has been used many times, but I would respectfully like to say that I am truly standing on the shoulders of giants. First, I'd like to share a bit about my mother's family. My mother's name is Agnes Concannon and she was born and reared in the village of Onaght on Inis Mor. It is the same village that we live in today.

I would like to mention a couple of deeply personal and important things about my mother's role in my life, since the day I was born, since my accident and up to this very day. There is an old song that says "A mother's love is a blessing "and I feel especially qualified to concur with the veracity of those fine words as that noble sentiment means the world to me. In truth, I would not be sitting here typing, enjoying the life I do or in reality, be the man I am, if it wasn't for my mother's love, fortitude, loyalty and her refusal to give up on me. I mentioned in Chapter 1, that my childhood accident has influenced and dictated the path of my life, but it has also brought my mother's life in a particular direction because of her love for me.

As I write these words, I am painfully aware of how inadequate these words actually are in trying to describe all that my mother has done for me and how she not only gave me life, in a very literal way, she continues to give me life on a daily basis. Like a lot of mothers, she has never sought any form of thanks or recognition but here I am, sitting at a keyboard attempting to put into words the impossibly deep set of feelings that I have for this amazing woman for putting my needs, desires and dreams ahead of her own. Again, I know the words are inadequate and do little justice to my mother – I would like to state and express my heartfelt love and thanks to her.

I would like to introduce the other members of my family as well and am reminded of a trip that I once took with my father. My father Bertie had a trawler at the time called The Girl Cliodhna. She was at the docks in Galway and she needed some work carried out on her in Killybegs up in Donegal. To make a long story short, it was decided that I would travel with my father in the trawler up to Killybegs in Donegal. It was a memorable trip and in the same way as most things in life, my memories are mostly and ultimately good but also sometimes a bit mixed. I can vividly remember being up in the wheelhouse of the boat with my father, and the feelings I had standing there beside him were of love, security and trust. My father is a big strong man and his ability and knowledge of the sea could only make you feel secure to be with him at sea.

Even though words of love did not pass between us, I have come to a point in my life where I can now recognize how much my father loved his son who happened to be disabled. Reading and seeing the subtle loving signs that I didn't notice in my younger years, but I can now see and more importantly feel, how this big strong man of the sea had and has as much love for me as the ocean has water.

That time on board The Girl Cliodhna (who was named for my sister), is a standout memory for me and while I was certainly, warmly and securely impacted by being at sea with my father, I must confess that I also had to deal with a set of feelings that were initially hard. I asked myself, "what if I hadn't had that accident? What would my journey be?"

Would I be out at sea with my father and be like my people before me, would I be farming like my mother's people, would I live abroad, would I have a family? The list is endless, and in truth there are no answers to those questions. On a good day they can be happy and idle ponderings but on a bad day they can be pure torment until I can gain some degree of acceptance. I know, for sure, that I am not the only one that asks these types of questions about my life. I know that every human being has their own version of these questions. I often have to think about these unanswerable questions and whereby I know that I don't have any secrets or hidden powers in dealing with them, I know in my heart of hearts that in everyone's lives, there are positives and negatives and whichever one we feed is the one that grows. Yes, I probably got a tough hand to play. I accept that I cannot answer all the questions about my life's path and the danger here is that in staying in fantasy as opposed to reality it would have two certain outcomes. I would either feel sorry for myself or it would stunt and restrict my growth opportunities.

I have learned to look past words and have developed a happy way of seeing what is in someone's heart – that has been liberating for me in my external relationships and more importantly, in my journey to self-acceptance and contentment in my own skin. I will write a little about my family on both sides as they have influenced and helped shape me into who I am today.

My mother's people are the Concannon's from the village of Eonaght towards the western end of this island. The Concannon's were and are, entrepreneurs, innovators, thinkers and doers. They have been blessed with being able to see life from a very global perspective. They are deep thinkers and very caring people. One of their outstanding and defining characteristics is their love for doing things differently and in their own way – they are creative, independent and possess a unique and generous spirited world view. In previous generations, they travelled from their Inis Meain home, saw the world and some might say, and conquered the world.

The spirit of these original thinkers has been an ever-present feature and positive influence in my life to date and this unusual and independent streak has helped me on so many occasions in the past. My mother's mother was called Mairin Concannon (nee Fleming), she was a national schoolteacher, a farmer's wife, a loving mother and grandmother and was also a niece of the famous island author Liam O Flaherty and indeed, a niece of his brother Tom too – another gifted writer. I have a flood of wonderful memories of her and distilling them down to a few sentences is both a labour of love and a limited snapshot.

All of my memories of this special woman are those of a grandson and while I am lucky enough to have a full and treasured memory bank of my Mamo, I find that every time I smell brown bread baking, that evokes the most beautiful and tender memories of my grandmother baking brown bread. In my mind's eye, I can clearly see her making the sign of the cross on the bread with a knife before she put it in the oven. This brown bread and so much more provided needed nourishments for her large family, and while it had a practical use, her real gift to her family was her love, support and loyalty.

I am blessed to still feel her influence in my life today and her legacy of love is priceless to me and an endless resource. My memories of my two grandfathers and my father's mother are a little bit jumbled but they come from my heart, nonetheless. If I'm honest, I was probably closer to my mother's mother – Mairin – than any of the others but certainly loved all four of them deeply. Like everyone else in life, I loved them all in a different way and enjoyed a different relationship with each one and consequently, was impacted, influenced and inspired by each one in their own unique way.

I was walking down by the football field in my own village and initially my mind wandered back to being down there years ago with my Uncle Eamonin on the tractor and cutting back briars. For no particular reason that was apparent to me, I started thinking about both my grandfathers and the men they were to me. My father's father was called Tommy Faherty. He was a tall, quiet and kind man. I remember him always wearing breidin trousers and using a rope as a belt - his dog, Shandy, was often with him. He was a hardworking man. My brother, Donal, used to be with Tommy a lot, moving cattle and bringing water to them. There was a red and black bench at the front of the house, and I clearly remember him sitting there with his stick beside him and with, more often than not, his dog. I can't say that I had many long heart-to-heart conversations with him but the legacy he left me was fed to me by his example. If he gave me nothing else, he gave me the priceless gift of loving and appreciating nature and the natural ways. This legacy was freely given to me by my two grandfathers and while it wasn't actually given with words, the actions, love and importance of these gifts could not have been any more powerful. I carry these treasures with me on a daily basis.

I have no doubt that these rare and treasured gifts got me through many difficult and painful times. There may be a form of mystery to me receiving these gifts but in truth, once I could step out of the way and stop blocking their path, these gifts from all 4 grandparents enriched my life beyond the words that I have.

My mother's father was called Eamon Concannon. He was always very nicely dressed and well turned out. Farming and family were his two passions. I remember moving cattle with him, and he'd ask me to block off a lane way to stop the cattle running up there. This made me feel very important and it felt wonderful to help him. I was always very happy to give him a hand when he asked me. Those thoughts happily and randomly visited me, and I am delighted to have those treasured memories and glad to share them. My father's mother was called, Nonie Faherty (nee Flaherty), also a native of this island - the village of Gortnag Capaill on the southern shore of this island. She had a very strong work ethic and was very good humoured. She kept students during the summer, knitted Aran Sweaters and smiled a lot.

At Easter - a beautiful memory comes to my mind - she always used to buy boxes of Easter Eggs and keep them in the back room for us. As kids we loved and devoured them and as an adult I value and appreciate her kindness and warmth to us all. The legacy from all my grandparents is priceless and no money could come near to buying it --- their values, generosity and love are the moral compass that my family and I live by today. I am blessed with a large, warm and loving extended family and in truth I could probably fill a complete book about them all and their lives, but I will limit myself to mentioning my 3 siblings; Rory, Donal & Cliodhna.

Writing about how much they mean to me and how important they are to me is something new for me and probably for them too. As I mentioned at the beginning of this chapter in the context of my home island – the community is at the very heart of this beautiful and rugged island, and for sure, family is the essence of community and is its very lifeblood. Accident or no accident, I would not be who I am today and certainly would not have been able to face my challenges without my family's love, commitment and support. I am fairly sure that Rory, Donal nor Cliodhna would actually know the extent that they have helped me, and I feel pretty sure that I would not have faced my challenges and fears without them. I read a quote one time, which went roughly like this: "Family isn't important – it is everything ".

Around 1991, from left to right, Ronan (age 16), Rory, Agnes, Donal, Cliodhna & Brutus (the dog)

Rory lives in America now, and even though I miss him terribly, I am so satisfied to see him as happy as he is. He works as a chiropractor and while I am not 100% sure, I feel that my childhood accident may have informed and influenced the direction of his work life to an extent. With no disrespect to my other siblings, Rory has always been a sort of a hero of mine – as his younger brother, I always looked up to him, but now as an adult, he is still every bit as much my hero as ever. His marriage to Kari inspires me on a daily basis and while I often feel lonely in myself, I am forever and always happy for my big brother.

Donal is my younger brother and he also lives on this island. Donal and I enjoy a great friendship and the bonus is, that we are brothers. Donal has the wonderful warm nature and every single person he meets in life feels his warmth and kindness. His natural instincts are to be kind and generous spirited, infectious in his positive and kind ways. We have never discussed it but in the same way that I look up to my older brother Rory, I also look up to my younger brother, Donal – in my heart of hearts, I quietly and silently hope that they both see me in the same loving light.

Finally, I have only one sister, Cliodhna and I would not be stretching it in saying that she is as beautiful on the inside as she is on the outside. Like a lot of families, I feel that Cliodhna is probably unaware of how much I care for her and value her. I am very happy and blessed to be able to share what Cliodhna and I share which is a wonderful friendship, and even though I have never actually thought about it up till now – Cliodhna has always been there for me, and to be honest that says so much about my little sister's character and values.

I have attempted to give a brief insight into the main people in my life and I'm not sure that I've done them justice, but I hope so. As I previously mentioned – when I used to write my blog, I always used to like to finish with a quote and I'd like to do that now to finish off this chapter.

"Never confuse a single defeat, with a final defeat."

~F. Scott Fitzgerald

Chapter 4

"Life is about progress, not perfection."

~ George Meehan

As I am writing my own story, I am glad that a certain amount of time has elapsed. I feel if I were to have written this 10 years ago that my emotions and feelings may have been too raw, and I don't feel that I would have had the necessary objectivity to tell my story. While my passion and feelings are absolutely there, the passing of time has allowed me to have a better handle on it all. Sometimes when I read back my own story, it can almost feel like I'm writing about someone else but then after a very short while I find myself back in the mindset and feelings of the little boy who was trying to come to terms with and make sense of what was truthfully a difficult situation.

As I mentioned before about the difference in giving out a blow by blow medical report and writing my personal story --- well, there is also a difference from a personal point of view in being in a medical coma with doctors telling my family that there was no hope and experiencing the power of familial love and having people with me, who just wouldn't give up and were never going to take no for an answer. I would not be writing this story if no for those loving and brave people who put my recovery first and loved me over the line to the life I enjoy today.

I was is a coma and not responding to any medical treatments or stimuli. People can draw their own conclusions as to what force was finally able to pull me back to life, but I know what I believe. My grandmother – Mairin Concannon, who had no medical background, experience or insights had her own ideas on what was needed. She taped my childhood friends from my national school on an old cassette player and played it to me as I lay in a coma. Now, there is no medical textbook that will say that the voices would or should have stimulated me or impacted, but they did.

There are volumes written about love conquering the unconquerable. I am happy to let those better qualified and with more experience than me make scientific arguments, but I can personally report that I was stimulated by the voices of my childhood friends and even though I can't give a logical explanation, the exuberant voices of my childhood friends provided me with a motivation and stimulation that goes beyond medical text books. Happily, it was the start of a meaningful recovery for me.

After I started showing signs of life, the medical team decided that it would best for both myself and my family if I were transferred to Galway to continue my recovery and even though there were most definitely many strains and stresses put on my family with the trauma of having a son in a coma – the transferring of their little boy to hospital in Galway, and closer to home, made it somewhat easier.

I am aware that when I moved to hospital in Galway that the burden of traveling as far as Dublin was removed from my family and one of the very first things that happened was that my next-door neighbour, and my best friend Denis came in to Galway to see me. He was brought to the hospital by his own mother, Maggie and it was very important to Denis to come in and support his friend. However important it was for the very young and very caring Denis – it was vital for me and his act of kindness at such a tender age and his familiar voice stimulated me in a way that was to have a lasting effect and influence and expedite my recovery.

How do you say thanks to such people – the words seem so inadequate and I feel they do not do justice to the innocent passion of a young boy who gets up in darkness, travels to Kilronan to get the steamer to Galway to show support, solidarity and care for his friend.

My recovery in Galway kept going from strength to strength – aided and abetted in no small part by the love I received from my family and my island community. People like Denis and my grandmother definitely started the ball rolling, but I was still in a pretty bad way and one of my many challenges was to learn to walk again. This process was very slow and very difficult for me and my family and the job in getting me on to my own two feet was ultimately going to prove to be too big a job for the poor medics in Galway. After several years of hospital and home recovery near Galway, it would eventually be decided that to get the treatment that would help me to walk again and give me the best chance at being independent, my treatment should continue up in the national rehabilitation hospital in Dún Laoghaire, Dublin. But before I describe that part of my recovery, I would like to describe how the consequences of my accident were impacting on my family.

Like a lot of real life situations my recovery and my accident seriously impacted on others as much, if not more than myself and if I were to just give out the medical facts, it would not be my story and could realistically be put in a couple of pages. It may not always appear to be the case, but I have always been aware of the seismic and lasting impacts that my accident had on my family and those close to me. It can very often present initially as a burden to me but as I firmly believe --- we are not responsible for the first thought that comes into our heads, but we are for the second ones.

I have learned over the years that despite the first thought very often being a sad or difficult one, that I can't afford to stop and dwell at that point and need to acknowledge the pain and sadness but not stay stuck there or I am going to struggle to keep going. The process has been that when the initial thought that my accident may well have burdened my family, the following thoughts and awareness's are; how much I am loved, valued and supported by my family, friends and community. Even as a very young boy, I had these sometimes-painful awareness's but as mentioned life has shown me how to deal with them – in any event, my family moved from Aran to Connemara and while culturally and geographically Connemara is close to my native island --- it's not home.

Both my parents come from large families and have been on these islands for generations and enjoyed a rich tapestry of family and community relationships that run very deep and are more important than I'm able to describe, they both put the welfare of their sick child and upped sticks and moved to Connemara to help me. I know it was never in their plan to move off their home island and while my Father was doing what he knew --- fishing, to provide for his family. He would have been out at sea a lot and even though his love for his family is the same as my mother's it's probably fair to say that the day to day consequences fell more on her shoulders. She never ever complained or said that she didn't want to leave her home island and the irreplaceable closeness of her family – she didn't hesitate for a second in doing what she could for her child. I feel very deeply the savage and brutal wrench that my mother went through in leaving her family for a new life over in Connemara which certainly was never her plan. As mentioned, none of this was lost on me as a child and even though I am supposed to have a brain injury – the sacrifices of my family were appreciated by me as much then as they are today.

My father was fishing his boat called The Albatross, and as a result of living in Connemara, he was now in Rossaveal a lot more than his home port on Aran. His working life changed significantly to facilitate his sick child's needs and possibly the crew were impacted too. The instinctive love that a parent has for their child was evidenced by both my parents in different ways and neither of them uttered a negative word.

My brother Rory, who I really looked up to and idolized – and still do - had to leave the national school that he attended on the island and where my grandmother taught and had to move to Connemara. He showed amazing maturity for such a small boy in realizing that his sick younger brother needed help and treatment. His maturity and bravery at that age has always been seen as an act of love by me and is a priceless treasure that has got me through some dark times. I would have been in hospital and Rory was attending the boys national school in Spiddal, I remember my mother used to collect Rory from school on her way to go to me in hospital --- not only would she have had his dinner on a plate in the glove compartment of the car, she would have had my younger brother Donal in a basket on the back seat. While my story may not be unique, I think it does permit me to say; A Mother's Love is a Blessing.

One of the constants that I have found to be true that has come about as a direct result of writing this book is; while we are culturally programmed to believe that everything in life is either black or white, I am certain that its more gray than either black or white and I am consistently finding that as I write and remember any particular time in my life, the memories are mixed. What I am genuinely trying to give an insight to is that gray, mixed and uncertain place --- some may call it the human condition and in truth, I wouldn't argue with that.

29

One stand-out memory from that period of time, is that I used to be able to visit home on a Sunday. While I really looked forward to those visits – they were classically mixed. I loved getting home to have a dinner made by my mother, loved to watch my big brother, Rory, kicking the ball outside in the yard, loved the homely smells and the absence of that hospital smell of anti-septic – which incidentally , every time I get that smell anywhere it evokes mixed memories that are probably more sad than happy, my associations of that normal smell can be powerful.

In any event, I lived for these visits at that time and found the sense of loneliness as I left the warm embrace of my family on a Sunday evening, very hard to take and often had trouble reconciling my range of thoughts. Often in my young mind on a Sunday evening I would resolve not to go home the next Sunday as the pain of leaving my family was almost unbearable but not unlike a lot of human situations, by the following morning, I was back to looking forward to and indeed living for my visit home. Even at a very young and tender age, while I missed my family in a way a child only can, I knew somewhere deep inside that I needed to be in hospital to continue my recovery which at that stage was painfully slow – in a literal sense.

I was receiving dedicated and up to the minute medical help in the hospital in Galway and while there is no doubt that without it, I could only dream of my life today, but once again consistent with the theme of mixed feelings and grey areas – the unshakeable and powerful love that I received from my family, friends and community was, I think, the factor that made all the difference.

In one way, I was unfortunate to experience the savagery of being knocked down and being badly and lastingly injured – one of the joys and irreplaceably positive outcomes is; how love can conquer all and literally give life. They say that the universe loves a stubborn heart, now, I can't honestly explain this, but I was and

30

am blessed to be surrounded by a range of stubborn and good hearts.

THE DYING WHALES

Mournful cry under the waves as
mammal is slaughtered for its
skin, flesh and all the rest is put to
waste while blood spills,
polluting sea.

A cry sends tears to heart as
whales gets caught in fishing nets
and twisting to break free dies in
mortal agony.

Lonesome sound sends tears to
eyes as whale is killed in ocean
deep, murdered in redding sea to
feed the greed of man.

Terrified orphan in the blue
beneath struggling to survive dies
in mortal agony.

As whales die in a blood red sea
for short term gain, it's future
endangered in our ocean blue.

By Ronan Faherty

Chapter 5

"Life is a long lesson in humility."

~ James M. Barrie

As I mentioned in the previous chapter, I was based in the Regional Hospital in Galway and going home on a regular basis. It's a strange and odd situation when you are in the company of medics and various caring family members, to have them discuss your welfare, your well-being, your recovery - in short, your life – right in front of you. I was under no illusions that every person was there for my benefit but sometimes I just wanted to scream as the difficulty was that in reality they couldn't really consult me, but I so wanted to have my say. Being a disabled man, being present when people discuss my life is something that I now understand better and find that over the years, I have become quite philosophical about seeing people's hearts and understanding their good intentions.

Having said all that, I am a human being with the normal range of feelings, fears and hopes and sometimes I can get very frustrated from being locked into this prison. This is one of my daily challenges in life and getting through it, invariably impacts on my quality of life and on my relationships.

I remember very well being in the hospital in Galway and while I can factually remember and report on my medical recovery, what is burned into my memory and is etched on my heart is how much I missed the normal and everyday parts of family life. I wanted more than anything, just be at home with my family – taking the good with the bad instead of being in an institution but life had dictated otherwise and I'm thinking of a song that a great Connemara singer sang once. His name is Bartley O'Donnell (or Beairtle Ó Domhnaill) and he sang the words "every man must bear his load". My load visited on me and my family in a most lastingly cruel and merciless way, but our collective challenge has been to deal with the facts and make as good a recovery as possible, while at the same time – not allow the consequences of the accident define us or make us in to someone that we aren't.

Going back to those lonely days in the hospital, one thing that had started to happen was that my visits home were becoming more frequent and for longer periods. These journeys home were difficult because my body was still pretty badly twisted, and I was essentially continuously in spasm and limited mostly to a wheelchair. One of the main reasons that enabled these visits home for me, was community spirit and pure human kindness.

A group of local women came to our house, sometimes 3 times a day, and with no medical background, but hearts full of love and a willingness to go through the pain barrier themselves, worked together to complete the necessary physical therapy with my body. These noble women put a sick child's needs before their own and I remember vividly being a small boy with what felt like useless, spastic limbs being pulled and stretched with love. A big piece of plywood was cut to be placed on the kitchen table, with leatherette at the edges, and it was the treatment table where the magic occurred. My mother would often have been sitting on top of me as these saints went about their difficult task of putting life and form back into my body.

I can never express enough gratitude to the all the doctors and medics, but what occurred in Spiddal with these amazing women was a form of miracle that was completely driven by human kindness and love. I am sure that I may be leaving some out, and I sincerely apologize for that, but I feel it to be very import that I not only mention these brave, dedicated and beautiful women but that I also thank them from the bottom of my heart for the priceless gifts they gave me through their love, fortitude and sweat. Some of these wonderful women are Nancy, Caitriona, Rose, Peggy, Mary, Martina, Sally, and my mother's sisters Nessa, Angela & Emer.

I remember feeling their love and dedication even though I probably didn't understand it fully at that time, I also remember crying in pain and through my child's tears, I can clearly see these loving, strong yet gentle women's faces and if there is such a thing as love in action, I was getting it by the bucket load from these angels. Their treatment of me was both healing and nourishing. At each of these sessions there was a huge feeling of love and recovery but also ever present at every single session was my mother, Agnes.

There are times in life when words are adequate and do justice to a situation, but I fear that words fall painfully short in this instance. The dedication and courage shown by these women deserves more thanks than I could ever give. As limited as these words may be, I still would like to offer my sincere thanks that through their courage and sweat, they eventually got my little body in to much better shape than when they started work on me.

All throughout my life and recovery there seems to be two parallels running side by side and essentially, they are my medical treatment and recovery alongside my family's love, dedication and refusal to give up on me. I can't really separate their impact on my life, and in truth, I wouldn't want to, but both have been essential to my recovery and both are the reason that I enjoy the quality of life that I do.

I know there is a huge movement towards Community care these days in terms of people's recoveries, but I am a direct product of community care. Community care, human kindness and love in a way that will probably never be written into any medical book but is a direct link to our ancient Celtic past whereby the more vulnerable members of our society were always looked after. These wonderful women gave me a great gift and part of my task and purpose in life is to find some way to pass that on and to keep it going. In truth, as I'm human – some days, I manage this better than others.

Another memory that I have, and to be honest a lot of the memories connected to my family at this time are quite mixed, in that I feel happy to accept their love and support, at the same time I couldn't help but feel that even though it wasn't my fault, that the consequences of my childhood accident impacted on my family in hugely significant way.

A memory that is in my mind in the vivid picture of my older brother, Rory watching and observing my treatments and recovery. I can clearly picture him in the house in Spiddal watching as the neighbours and friends tried and succeeded in straightening out my twisted body. I can't be 100% sure how much this impacted on my brother or if it influenced his decision to become a chiropractor – he now lives in America and heals people for a living, but I feel deep down that it is his vocation and true calling. Did those early sessions play a small part – I would like to think yes, they did.

My only sister Cliodhna, was present for so many of these treatments and was on this journey in a very real sense and again, I don't think it is a coincidence that Cliodhna has wonderful healing gifts and qualities also. These two examples both have gotten me through some darker times, and I rejoice in the people that they have become and if anything good can possibly be salvaged from my accident – well, that has got to a strong part of it.

The community care and the hospital care, both successful in their own right, came to a natural conclusion in that I couldn't really be helped any further in either place – however well intentioned.

Around the age of 15, the decision was made that the next part of my recovery needed to take place in the National Rehabilitation Hospital in Dun Laoghaire, Co Dublin. Before I write about the next part of my recovery, I would also like to relay that the ominous and sick feeling in my stomach at the thought of another move and another change, filled me with a huge amount of fear and sadness.

1990, age 15. Our house in Pairc Thoir in Spiddal.

I was certainly discussed as I lay there, and I cried many a bitter tear in my hospital bed at the thought of more upheaval for myself and my family. All the tears in the world could not stop the next phase of my recovery, which was absolutely necessary and vital to me. My childish and naive resistance was mostly in my own mind and I'm afraid to say that in this instance I honestly wouldn't have been aware of what was in my best interest. Off I went to the National Rehab as I need twice daily intensive sessions of physiotherapy for my twisted body, and again, I was to meet a number of saints on my journey.

When you come from a small island community, people do a lot more than pay lip service and I happily got visits from so many Dublin based island people – I'll never forget their kindness. During my nearly 2 year stay in the National Rehabilitation Hospital, I was living in a gate lodge with up to 6 kids at a time and we were looked after in a very motherly and caring way by Sister Angela, who was our quasi parent and teacher.

I felt like I had literally been ripped away from my family and even though it broke my heart, as a child you tend to adjust to whatever the circumstances are – I missed my family every minute of every day. Sister Angela gave so much love to me and the other kids in her care that while it didn't fix my broken heart, it did make my life much better.

I was and am very fortunate to have the mother I have – she came up to Dublin every week to spend time with her sick little boy. Many kids do adjust quite quickly but I lived to see my mother's face and her presence was better than 100 physio sessions. During her visits to Dublin to see me, she used to stay across the road from the Hospital with a priest – like a lot of parts of my recovery story, this happened unofficially and outside of the system and my view today is that the care my mother received was

Christian, compassionate and supportive. I'm not sure that it would happen today.

I was eventually to get out of the wheelchair in Dun Laoghaire and somewhat shakily onto my own to legs and that was a massive step for me in every sense. Even though I spent nearly 2 years in Rehab, I was so fortunate in that I used to get the chance to spend a good part of the summer with my family on our home island.

The feeling in my heart at the thought of going home to my family was one thing, but added to that, we were coming home to the island. It was an overload of sorts for me and I experienced pure joy and a wild happiness.

A few things stand out in my memory from that time. I remember getting a 3-wheeler bicycle and when I made my first ride, what may have appeared to be a simple cycle was a massive journey to me and represented independence, freedom and a huge achievement. I was very aware at the time that my cycle was seen in its enormity by my family and my community – this made me feel great.

I was also given the gift of a donkey by a very wise and intuitive neighbour, Sean. He is an astute and insightful man and knew that by having this donkey that I would care for him, exercise him and feed him, while at the same time being the primary beneficiary of this transaction. A kind act by a decent man who knew the psychology of recovery.

On my first trip home to our island I made my First Holy Communion with my old school friends. I wouldn't have been able to express at the time how much it meant to me to back amongst my own people but the feelings running through me were as strong as I've ever felt. Feeling a sense of community, belonging and identity was nearly overwhelming even at such a tender age. I can't be sure if it was as a direct result of my accident and subsequent recovery experiences or not but being home was very much a happy state of mind as much as a physical presence.

The end of the second summer came, as did my stint in The National rehab, and next it was back to Connemara for myself and my family for an attempt at mainstream education.

Chapter 6

"Your time is limited, so don't waste it living someone else's life."

~ Steve Jobs

In the previous chapter I mention how I was attending Mainstream school in Spiddal National School. I have mixed memories of my time there and indeed of my journey to get there.

We lived about a mile away from the school and the culture at that time would have been very much that children walked places. Now, I find myself reluctant to over-emphasize this, but I guess a big part of my story is about being different. In any event, there came a day when I was able to walk from our house to the National School in Spiddal. This was a huge achievement and that walk was facilitated by my family and the dedication of the women of Spiddal who stretched and loved me over the line with their loving physio and dedication. I walked to school and felt a glorious sense of freedom and independence. At this time my greatest wish was just to be like everyone else and making that walk made me feel part of the world I lived in. This would soon change.

Even though I could walk to school and at times take the bus, the harsh reality was, that I wasn't coping in mainstream education. I really wanted to fit in, blend in and be one of the boys, but it wasn't to be. I wasn't coping educationally, physically or socially.

I remember very well, when the bell for our break would sound, all the kids would be brim full of youthful exuberance and would rightfully go tearing out the door into the yard. I watched them run past me one by one and because of my twisted limbs, I couldn't run with them as my heart desired and I experienced for the first time, feelings of anger, jealousy and the pain of being different.

These were alien feelings to me, and I honestly didn't know how to cope or process them. I instinctively knew that turning my negative feelings on myself would not help me, but this is exactly how that firstly manifested itself and I found myself facing a dilemma, do I feel different and limited and feel sorry for myself or do I somehow embrace the fact that while I may well be different, I am alive.

I am not going to paint an overly rosy picture and claim that I immediately found and embraced the healthy path. I didn't. I initially felt very angry and upset but these were not entirely useless feelings as they served me in being a catalyst of sorts that facilitated me in looking at myself and accepting who I was and am. This process initially brought me to some dark and angry places but even though I was young, I was cruelly faced with having two blunt choices - accept myself and grow, or deny myself and regress.

Eventually, I chose to accept and embrace who I was and alongside my young dilemmas and soul searching, it was decided by a combination of my family and the teachers that my needs would not be served by attending mainstream school. As I was coming to the point whereby I could accept that I was different and somewhat limited, the next part of my educational and personal journey was to take place in a "special school".

I came to several realizations at that time; I had slowly come to realize that I was actually different, and I didn't fit in to mainstream schooling but getting there was a difficult, painful and at times, a very fearful process. Part of me ached to just be a normal little boy who could run out the door when the bell for break sounded, but for better or worse; I had reluctantly come to the point where I was more and more comfortable with being different from the other boys in Spiddal School.

The first day that I went into the special school on the grounds of Merlin Park Hospital in Galway City, I felt a strange and unfamiliar feeling - that I wasn't different. I was with people who for a variety of reasons and from a variety of backgrounds, also had special needs and who also didn't fit in to mainstream education.

I experienced for my first time that I was with like-minded people who were kindred spirits. It gave me a very secure feeling and in the same way that negative and harsh realities forced me to deal with my reality, these surprising feelings of identification gave me a feeling of finally belonging and however I got here, I was finally with my own kind and it felt ok. I realized that, being different isn't the worst thing that can happen in life and that being angry, jealous and having no acceptance of one's circumstance is a fate much worse.

1993, Age 18. My schoolmates at Holy Family School on a trip.

Strangely enough, one of the options that I thought about was giving up altogether and it looked attractive for a brief period. I also knew that people would understand if I gave up and in a well-intentioned and loving way, would facilitate me giving up and in ways excuse it.

When I arrived in the special school it was a turning point for me and I enjoyed being in a class with people of different ages who had all walked a crooked road to get here too and if anyone deserved and earned their seat in that class room, these fine people did. Now, I know that no more than myself these people would shun praise and detest pity but the potency of being with these lovely people was to change my life.

I eventually progressed on to the Training Centre and was with an entirely new group of people. My experience in starting in the special school really stood out to me and I found this transition much easier and more natural. One particular memory I have is listening to the unique and beautiful stories of each person at the school. I wouldn't consciously have been looking for identification at this time but a very big by product of going to this Training Centre was, that I was really getting a deep level of identification and thus self-acceptance. Even though I didn't go to the Training Centre to find those qualities, it turned out to be the start of what was to be a lifelong process in encountering negatives and working through them to the point whereby they actually be positives.

Going to the mainstream school was a mixed experience for me in that it was my heart's desire to be attending school just like everyone else and to be treated and dealt with like everyone else. While I gleaned a certain amount of joy and satisfaction from being in the mainstream school it also had the effect of giving me a harsh and somewhat cruel awakening – I was probably as much delusional as I was hopeful. Life was to intervene as it very often does, and those stark and uncomfortable realizations were to be the beginning of my struggle for self-acceptance. I would like to think and feel that my victory over negative, painful and difficult feelings only go to cement a lack of acceptance and are guaranteed to give no peace of mind or quality of life.

What presented in a very painful and unwelcome package was to prove to be my catalyst in facing my realities. One outcome that I would like to share in relation to facing realities, is that in my direct experience, the thoughts of facing it are much worse that actually grasping the nettle and facing the difficulties. I didn't immediately get this and like a lot of people, I went to great lengths to avoid facing my own painful reality and this was like a death by a thousand cuts. The more and more I avoided my truths, the further and further away were my chances of making a meaningful recovery.

Even though I have never been to prison, at that time I felt totally imprisoned, primarily driven by my own lack of acceptance. This was a very lonely time and I felt very lonely, different and isolated. I was in this broken body and I was crying inside just to have a normal life and be like everyone else. What I couldn't see at the start of this process was that the more entrenched I became in the fantasy and wishing my life away, the less chance I had of living my own life and being the person that I knew I could be and wanted to be.

In a strange and very liberating way, when I was forced to leave mainstream education, even though it burst my bubble in some regards, it also led me onto the path of self-acceptance and recovery.

Again, it was a strange feeling to be at the point whereby I could comfortably and reasonably accept that while I definitely had limitations – there was no way that I was going to let them define me as a person or dictate how I felt about myself. These conclusions gave me a great sense of myself but were also a bit scary, as I didn't really know what to do with this new-found knowledge and awareness that I had so painfully acquired. Fortunately, these realizations and awareness's coincided in a general way with my attendance at the Training Centre and in a very practical way, I was feeling very comfortable there and most definitely felt less stigmatized.

I look back on the period that I spent in the Training Centre as a happy time. I was learning new skills daily and internally I was feeling ok about being me, and all that entailed. I was very eager and almost sponge like with all the new opportunities to learn and develop – we learned; baking, upholstery, woodwork and gardening.

I found that I really enjoyed the indoor pursuits and activities best and while that is a simple enough sentence to write, it was a little bit of a trauma, as usual, in allowing myself permission to reach that conclusion. Part of my process was initially torturing and tormenting myself with thoughts like "I am the first member of my family that hasn't worked the land or the sea, and if I had never had my accident, would I have been out fishing with my father or farming with my grandfather and uncles". Now, I understand that these thoughts are perfectly natural and normal, but my own personal danger lay in staying stuck on those thoughts and vainly searching for an answer to questions that just can't be answered.

Would I have been fishing or farming? Who knows. It is a question that there is no answer to and more than that, it is a form of quick sand in that to stay stuck at that point, one could sink.

I mainly write about my process to show that my initial thoughts were rarely wholesome, life affirming or good for me, but I realized that I had a personal responsibility to acknowledge the initial negatives but to move to past them to a healthier place. This really has been and is a lifetime deal for me. Having talked with many able-bodied people over the years, I realize that my struggles are not unique, but they are my path and my choices to make.

I felt very productive and happy in the Training Centre. I was enjoying the day to day challenges but one thing I used to especially look forward to, was going on our day trips. I loved being on the bus and seeing new places and having new experiences – it was a great feeling to be travelling through the countryside and seeing all these wonderful sights that I had never seen before. Another aspect to being on the bus with the people from the Training Centre was, that they were pretty much operating at the same pace as myself – there was no body whizzing by me, inadvertently making me feel different and less than.

These were glorious, happy and fun filled outings to such places as Castlebar in Co Mayo and Dublin. Separate to the joy of the trips, I can clearly remember sitting on the bus feeling that along with my island community and family that these were my people and I comfortably belonged.

1992, Age 17. Leisure Dome in Galway

I was in a good place mentally at this stage and felt I was making good and reasonable progress in the Training Centre and probably, for the first time I felt contented with my lot. The physical constraints I had were ever present and while some day to day activities were more cumbersome than a lot of people would encounter, I found more and more that I was accepting my physical limitations with walking and using my hands. Even though the medics told me that I had a brain injury as well, this brain injury was something that I refused to have define me in any way. No body, including me, would want it but I once again I remember the words of a neighbour when he said, "everybody has a disability, it's just more visible in some than others".

I accepted and accept today that I have certain limitations, but they are by no means terminal. Another neighbour called Pat (or Bhertie), often used to say, "two things in life can trip you up; assumptions and presumptions". In a very literal way, I not only had to absorb those two valid statements – I had to live them.

One memory I have in relation to my time in the Training Centre was getting the bus home. Forgive me if I am writing about such a normal and perfunctory experience but a bus journey home was hugely representative and was a tribute in particular to my Mother's love and dedication to me. As I mentioned, I was blessed to have so many people with stubborn hearts and belief in me, that in some ways, I was a very rich man.

Community spirit is at the heart and is the essence of any area or group. I remember when I used to take the bus home. I was afraid of the dark and a neighbour who worked in Galway, and who used to get my bus, used to walk me home to the door as I was petrified of the dark. This man never sought praise, not to mind thanks. He was the father of Padraig O Ceidigh, founder and owner of Aer Arann. His kindness and similar kindnesses were something that I have been the fortunate recipient of on more than one occasion and I find one sincere challenge I face is, how do I pass that on?

My time in the Training Centre was now coming to an end and not unlike most people I was faced with the mixed emotions of excitement and fear about my next steps.

World of Conflict

Soldiers at war, fighting for their country,
living in horror and in pain, with visions from
the combat filling the minds of young with anger
and bloodshed and discomfort with cry
which can be heard all over the globe.

The echoing blasts of firepower is been
reported by media as innocent victims are bleeding and dying in
our streets and terrifying people run for protection from the battle
of gun fire.

As citizens of innocents are slaughtered
the weak is left behind to fight for them self, while struggling to
stay breathing, people are dying in the street, even as child's
suffering with no parents.

As terrifying victims flee for silence
from the cover of war, they go on a voyage
to some land beyond to start a new life.

With the fortress of this island where
the plea of the youthful was been
ended as the solders put in jeopardy life of
young and people of our advancing years.

By Ronan Faherty

Chapter 7

"We are all failures - at least, the best of us are."

~ James M. Barrie

My time in the Training Centre was a very happy time for me and even though I had spent practically every day of my life resisting and in a lot of ways, denying that I was different and had certain limitations - my time in the Training Centre allowed me to adjust in my own time and ultimately accept that I am different and do have limitations. I was most definitely fearful of facing these harsh and merciless facts, and in truth I did all sorts of mental acrobatics in my efforts to avoid the truth. I have often heard; the truth will set you free.

My direct life experiences bear that out, as once I stopped fantasizing and wishing my life away, I began to live my life in earnest. The net outcome was acceptance. I'm me. For better or worse this is who I am, and irrespective of how I got here, this is the hand of cards that I must play. As true as my name is Rònàn Ó Fatharta, I am going to take my place in the world and be me.

I am no different to anyone else on two levels at least; we all have our troubles and I have the same feelings, desires, hopes, dreams & fears as everyone else.

Up to this point in my life, while I really wasn't aware of it, every single person that I encountered in any environment was trying to help me, were kind to me and wanted the very best for me.

I got wonderful help at every single stage of my life and my gratitude runs deep. I know I can never honestly repay even a fraction of the help I received but upon leaving the Training Centre, I was as well-prepared skills-wise as I could be, and medically I had progressed beyond my own and my family's wildest dreams. I, like many before me, was leaving the safety and security that I had known up to that point and was heading into the harsh realities of the adult world. I was to quickly find out that I wasn't ready for it, but in truth I was only able for it in a limited way.

1992, age 17

One dream that I had, which was probably bordering on fantasy was - I wanted to live independently. My mother in particular really helped me with this goal in so many ways. I moved into a place near Galway City, which was a form of

52

sheltered accommodation but had no house parent. I was expected to be able to cook and fend for myself.

In reality, I was able to do neither and early every morning, my mother would drive across town to help me - she cooked for me and did all the stuff that I couldn't do. After a relatively short period of time, roughly 2 weeks, it was clear to everyone concerned that I was not a candidate for independent living. This was initially a bitter pill to swallow and was my first bubble burst after leaving the Training Centre.

I have no regrets about trying it and at this stage, feel no shame about it not working out, but in the initial aftermath of moving back home to my mother and sister, Cliòdhna, I must say, it felt like the end of the world on one level but on another level, I was glad to be going home.

Getting an initial feeling that something was the end of the world and a feeling of hopelessness was something that I would become familiar with. I learned how to take on board my initial feelings and fears, but also vitally learned that my initial feelings were reactions and driven by my fears and always had to be faced and worked through. In most cases, I have been able to work stuff through and make healthy choices and decisions, there are times that my reality can be merciless and all I can reasonably do is seek acceptance.

Acceptance for me is never a destination or one-time deal, it's usually a daily occurrence for me. Like a lot of people's life situations, I find a form of freedom comes with acceptance.

I was now living quite contentedly back at home with my mother and sister. They had moved in from Connemara to the outskirts of Galway City to facilitate me moving on to the next stage. I think it is fair to say that we all ached for and missed our island home and most of the time it was the elephant in the room.

In any event, with the help and support of my family, I managed to get a job in a local Supermarket as a shelf stacker. There were a number of familiar feelings that came with this job.

Like being in the Boys National School in Spiddal, I felt different and was struggling to cope physically, mentally & socially. I found a lot of everyday tasks quite difficult and I know that I dropped and broke merchandise on more than one occasion. I hated doing this and very often had to work very hard not to internalize the realities of my limitations and slaughter myself. My initial reactions were to beat myself up over these things but I knew I owed it to myself and my family not to indulge these feelings as they would not lead me anywhere good and would hurt the people I loved and who were so good and selfless for me.

I went about my work as best as I could and while the work was one thing, being in the staff canteen was a different thing altogether. While I was in there on my breaks, the one theme that was discussed more than anything was relationships. I loved hearing them discuss all aspects of their love lives and even though it was fascinating to me, I honestly had no experience of relationships. I really wanted first-hand experience. Who wouldn't want to love, to be loved, touch, to feel needed and to feel desirable? I longed for all these things and while I was in the staff canteen, I compulsively wanted to hear all about my work colleagues' love lives, it also left me feeling very isolated and lonely. I longed to be someone's special person and still do. I am slow to write this confession, but I've never had a relationship yet as I haven't been lucky enough to meet someone.

I went to a number of Christmas parties and even danced at the parties. Like a lot of events and occurrences in my life it was a mixed bag. I stayed working in the Supermarket for around 2 years but in truth I left as I wasn't coping on any level. Leaving the job was initially very difficult but again, I had a very serious responsibility to make this a positive and not allow the negative dimensions impact on how I felt and feel about myself.

During the next period of my life, I must admit that while I was going through it, it felt bleak and lonely. I am no different than anyone else in that while you are going through stuff it can be very hard to see the bigger picture.

My sister, Cliodhna, at this stage had moved to Jersey and it was just myself and my mother living in a housing estate on the outskirts of Galway. While this 2- or 3-year period was like treacle while I was going through it, I would like to think, looking back at it, that this process lead me onto the right path. There is most definitely a lesson there for me about trusting my process and taking off my blinders.

I was unemployed for this period of time. It would often get to me and I would feel lonely, unproductive, isolated and if I'm honest, I was even more aware of the fact that I was different and had limitations. I would, in time, learn to differentiate between limitations and barriers.

During this period, I had the opportunity to reflect and look at my life, and especially where I fitted in and where I didn't. I knew that I didn't fit into mainstream education, I knew that I didn't fit in to the workforce in the supermarket and while my initial feelings were to feel a bit helpless about this, what was to follow in the form of a series of small revelations was to change my life.

At every stage throughout my life, and most especially during periods that it was clear that I wasn't fitting in, in the back of my mind was my heartfelt and secure feeling that whether I fitted into mainstream education or not, whether I had work limitations or not, whether I was in a relationship or not, the undeniable fact was - I am an island man, first and foremost, and I fit in on my island home with my family, friends & community. I always have and I always will.

During my period of unemployment while myself and my mother were living in the outskirts of Galway, the realizations that I missed and belonged to my island home were as powerful as they were undeniable.

I wanted to go home. In all honesty, right at that moment that is all I knew, and I was 100% certain of that fact. They say, "every savage loves his native shore". This penny had finally dropped for me, and although I didn't know what to do with this vital information or how to go about making it happen, I knew I was going home.

Chilled Wind

Frozen gale gives us the cold-blooded crisp wintry chill, among thousand streams, swiftly the spring and summer pass us by white clouds the morning is still a cold night of snow upon first page.

Winter is snappy with chill and sharp shavers down the back and as I paused to her song, I saw and heard one sunny morn, while swift moment slide the earth was green and the sky was blue.

Who has seen the wind, neither you or I, but when the trees bow down there heads the breeze passing us by, thoughts lost, blowing through my mind like pockets of wind through my palms.

A fearsome wind cannot compel the weakest branch to gladly yield, howling like a wolf through the trees, we want the kind of love that makes sunsets seem like little sparks of fire, fading in the summer wind.

We are all who falls, like been pushed by the cyclone, you look like heaven but I look like hell, winter wind, Jack Frost Rain is all around and draft as well, it runs through fields and trees.

As the air lifted me up into upper atmosphere where we dance to the rhythm of the music to the tunes of the northern breeze frozen in timeless melody, howling like a wolf scattering leaves.
By Ronan Faherty.

Chapter 8

"The greatest pleasure in life is doing what people say you cannot do."

~ Walter Bagehot

In this chapter of my life, I had what started out as a little niggle about going home to my island and to be honest this niggle kept growing and growing every day, to the point where there were times it was all I could think about. It was around 1998 and I was in my early 20's. I wanted to go home, but I had no clue how I might go about or where even to start. My gut and my instincts were screaming at me to go home.

This period in my life, when myself and my mother were living outside of Galway, was a tough time for me. I have always had the habit of getting up early and even though this was a grim time in my life, I stuck very closely to my routine as it helped get me through to the next stage. I used to get up early and my mother used to go to work very early as she was cooking in an old folks' home.

I would get up early and similar to many other times in my life, my relationship with my dog was hugely important and significant to me. I would walk Brutus my dog, and even though there were many days that I didn't want to go out and very often would come up with the most plausible and reasonable reasons why I shouldn't go out walking with Brutus, I always did. To be honest, I never regretted it. Quite the opposite. Getting out for a walk and moving my limbs while in the open air was a Godsend.

I was out of work during this time and struggled quite a bit with boredom and having too much time on my hands. I found that it was vitally important to my mental wellbeing that I found the most positive ways possible to set my self-tasks that would fill the time and where possible keep my thoughts positive.

As the days were long, I must admit that there were times when I had to wrestle with dark thoughts. Some people call this stinking thinking, and I wasn't exempt from it but knew with every part of me that I couldn't afford to dwell in this unhappy place. I recognized it when it visited me and found myself to have become very disciplined and almost relentless about processing negative thoughts and feelings and being brutally honest with myself in order to keep in reality and reject fantasy. While fantasy was seductive in ways, similar to a sugar fix, it never did me any good and without exception, always made things worse for me.

So, I was highly motivated in doing my daily tasks. I would walk my dog Brutus every day. A lot of days I would get the bus into town and even though at times I would be manufacturing little jobs and tasks, it was most definitely a more positive action than sitting at home thinking. Another task that I worked into my day was walking with Brutus down to the old folks' home where my mother worked and we would walk home together. After a short period of time the residents of the old folks' home began to look forward to myself and Brutus' visits.

I encountered similar feelings to when I was in the special school and the Training Centre, in that the lovely folks in the home didn't judge me in any way and were very much at ease around me. Consequently, I was completely comfortable with them and if they looked forward to my visits, I certainly very much looked forward to visiting them. Somehow, they seemed to be able to see past my disability and just see me - I loved this.

They loved to see Brutus coming too and were always very affectionate and kind to him. I was very connected to Brutus and we had a wonderful friendship. These visits became a central part of my day and my life.

I also noticed that on our walks home, myself and my mother started talking more and more about our island home. I'm not sure that I would have admitted, even to myself, how much I was missing my island - primarily, I was afraid to go there as I feared it would never be a reality for me.

As the days grew into weeks and months and onto years, we talked and talked more and more of home, of family, of neighbours and friends. I am sure that my mother's heart was silently breaking and I'm sure that she was willing to go to any lengths to help her boy in whatever way she could. I knew in my heart of hearts that she would do anything and go anywhere to help me. In reality, we were both suffering in silence at missing our real home.

I felt that because of her true heart that she was never going to suggest it as she probably thought that I was in the best place to get on going help. This was possibly true on some levels but that huge and vitally important piece of the jigsaw that was our life was; we are island people through and through and we just wanted to be home with our own people. I was able to see and feel my mother's love for me and knew that because of her honour, she would never suggest going home.

To put it simply, I grabbed the initiative and said, "Mommy, I want to go home ".

This was a tearful and emotional event for both mother and son but finally we had put words to that elephant in the room and an ominous feeling left me and was replaced with a tingling feeling of excitement. Also, the deep sense of comfort you get when not only do you make the right decision, but you know you have.

Making the decision was a slow and fearful process but once it was made, things seemed to happen quite quickly for us. I can't really explain it but when you are doing the right stuff for the right reasons, the universe can very often align and facilitate this.

Finding out if my mother could get work on the island was a very important factor. At this particular time, an old folks' home was opened up on our island, thanks to some very dedicated and honourable islanders. To make a long story short, my mother was offered the position of cook in this new enterprise and home we were going.

The first period of time at home on our island was mixed to an extent, but definitely more good than bad. We were living in a rented house, which wasn't probably ideal, but we were at least on our home island and felt as though we had never left. It wasn't lost on me for one minute, how much my mother had missed her family and to watch her in their midst really filled my heart. My mother and I were surrounded by love, not just from both my parent's families but from our island community too.

I was out of work and kept the discipline of my daily walks. As I now had a fine 3-wheeler, I added daily cycles as well. The difference for me was that on my cycles or walks, I always met people to talk to and not only was I using my first language of Irish, I was in the heart of a caring community that always kept a watchful eye out for me. I was very comfortable to be in my own place with my own people and I believe this made a big difference.

Even though my walk was, and still is, bad, there was a spring in my step and a feeling of harmony in my heart. There was a lovely familiar feeling that you get when you put on a nice comfortable old sweatshirt - it just fits. I was in this place and had great feelings of being where I was meant to be.

Alongside this, I was still struggling to cope with unemployment and too much time on my hands. Similar to my mother landing a job in the old folks' home, my social worker managed to get me seasonal work up at the ancient and spectacular fort of Dún Aonghasa (anglicized Dun Aengus). I was and still am, working Monday to Friday for the office of public works for 4 hours a day up at the Fort.

There is a lot I like about this. I really like meeting people from all over the world, and have honestly met them from far and wide, and these experiences have enriched my life greatly. I also love the feeling when I finish my day's work of walking into a café or restaurant and ordering my lunch. It feels so good to do it as a working man and honestly it seems to taste better.

On a different level, I love the dignity of work, the feeling of being useful, I love having a structure and purpose in my day, week and life. There is a real difference in walking in to order a hot chocolate after my day's work to just wandering in and having one. I'm not sure that I can fully express that but it's very important to me.

During this period of time, we also managed to build a house on my mother's family land. There are 7 houses of my mother's family in our village and unlike being in the housing estate, when I open the windows or stand in the garden, one of the beautiful sounds that I can hear is my cousin, Orla's children playing. The youthful voices are magical and musical to me. This music seems to sing, "Welcome Home, Rònàn ".

I seem to feel more independent when I am on my home island having my walks and cycles. I can't say I was restricted in town but most definitely the feeling of belonging, of fitting in and just being home completed a lot for me. I know on the mainland that I was seen primarily as a disabled man but here, I was and am, just Rònàn. I love that.

I feel more accepted here and as a consequence, I feel I accept myself better too. Even though I have a brain injury and bad coordination, I feel better able to cope and deal with that here.

My dog Brutus is no longer around but I have a new little friend called, Elvis, named after my hero, who I walk with every day and with whom, I enjoy a great friendship. I feel very fortunate and grateful to have made it home. Not everyone does and in some ways my story could end here, but there is more.

MY BEST FRIEND

My dog is my mate who likes going on
walks, for the wag of a tail and a bark of
hello to run and to jump.

Our loyal, friendly face is happy when
they see a formulary facade of
companionship, our past dogs we miss
them all.

We saw a sigh at our vet, take me home,
help care for a friend, find a home help
him mind, we each have a breed that we
hold dear.

A memory lasts forever never dose it die,
true friends no matter their actions will
always care, our forever associates.

By Ronan Faherty

Chapter 9

"Family is not an important thing. It's everything."

~ Michael J. Fox

I had a variety of thoughts about how best to write this chapter and there were a number of drivers and motivators in making the decision which ultimately I made. I believe the best way to give an honest account of my families' point of view and experience is to let them tell it. It's probably a little bit like the guy who was having a chat with God about his life and pointed out to God that during the hardest times in his life that were only one set of footprints in the sand and he reasonably asked God if he had abandoned him during those tough times. No, said God, they were the times that I was carrying you.

On reflection, I think it's probably fair to say that for a lot of my life, I was carried – metaphorically, emotionally and very often physically. Even though, like everyone else, I have to determine my own happiness and wellbeing, I feel like I have had more love, support and compassion than anyone would ever dream possible.

I wanted to describe what it has been like for my siblings in particular, and was going to write out my version of their experience, but my sister Cliodhna has the wonderful and courageous idea that realistically and honestly, there was no one better qualified than themselves to write that piece and I have to say that I totally agree with her. While I hated asking them to do it as I felt it might have been a big ask – their responses couldn't have been more encouraging and I'm so glad that they have had the opportunity to share how it was for them.

The accident that I was involved in all those years ago changed my life forever and brought my life's journey in a particular direction, but what a lot of people may not always realize is, how events in our own lives can dramatically and lastingly affect our loved ones. I hope the pieces from my 3 siblings will give a different perspective to the journey that I have been on as a disabled man.

Rory's Story

Ronan has always been my little brother, and being close in age we hung out a lot. Bearing witness at the tender age of seven to my little brothers' accident was very traumatic and this trauma, or PTSD, has a strong memory connection for me. I can still to the day smell some of the smells, hear some of the noises, and remember both the scenes and people involved. Ronan was immediately flown off to the intensive care and remained in a coma for some time. Then came the period of grace as it slowed all our lives down. I remember the continual praying and anticipating Ronan's first response since his accident.

Now, being a parent myself of children, I could not have imagined what my mother and father were going through. We prayed to all the saints and gods we could think of to wake Ronan up from his slumber and to be part of our life again, but it wasn't until we played the tape cassette of Elvis, the king of rock 'n' roll, that his eyes opened, and a smile came back on his face again.

I've always contemplated the impact of Elvis and the role he played in our family and continues to play to this day. Both Ronan and my mother had visited Graceland to pay homage to our unlikeliest of heroes.

We were all happy that the bugger was finally awake, and we could get on with our lives as a family and as brothers to play and have fun. There was a little snag of course in that we then had to go through the period of rehabilitation.

The accident created limitations and unlike other children his age he could not do the things that typical children did. We have always been blessed that wherever we moved and lived, we had amazing neighbours and friends to help with Ronan with his ongoing treatments and care. When we lived in Spiddal, Co Galway for well over a year, we had a rotation of a spectacular group of mothers that would gather and perform a very specific passive exercise on my brother. We are eternally grateful to their care and service in which they had provided.

Our ongoing rehab surrounded by an awesome care team allowed Ronan an early foundation that he could build on to get his mind and body back. These early adaptations influenced me to where I am today. I got my bachelor's in biology and Doctorate in Chiropractic. I was fascinated by everything related to healing of the body and mind. While in college I got my certification in massage, exercise training and Bio Energy to name but a few. Ronan inspired me to take the career path I choose.

Ronan always grew up being accepted no different to anyone else. At times it was difficult to be present to his limitations, which often times would end in disappointments or painful accidents, which unfortunately were numerous. Such as wheelchair accidents, near drowning swimming pool incidents, indoor playing that would end up with someone's head through a window. This kid endured a lot. He was hardy and still is.

Ronan has a serious fondness of Elvis, loves to travel, loves M&M's (especially peanut ones), adores any electronics that pertain to Apple, and has a love of writing and poetry that I admire. He tends to be a deep thinker like the statue of the thinking man on a rock. I suppose growing up on an island with the environment we had, has an unavoidable impact on who we become. And finally, the guy has a great sense of humour with an infectious smile that draws you in. You cannot help but be curious about this legend. I am excited to see what we are creating for next chapter in our lives.
~Rory

Donal's Story

Some of my earliest memories involve my brother being stretched and straightened and given a huge amount of work by my mother and a group of fantastic women from the area in Spiddal over a number years, and then later in my youth of seeing this hard work progress to walks around the rural version of a block. My mom and her co-conspirators used to drag the rest of us kids along quiet often, if we wanted to go or not. Day by day, week after week, month after month Ronan endured therapy. Help from these good people with all this physical activity as well as brain training for memory, reading, and writing is not easy to forget.

I was quite young when the more intensive work was being done with Ronan, especially in regard to his physical ability and mobility. As I grew, I thought this was completely normal. The first time maybe that I got a bit of a hint to the otherwise was my first day in primary school. Ronan would've been in the fourth class before secondary school because of the age difference, so in I walked thinking my older brother was going to have my back at school, cracking the odd smart comment or joke and being the centre of attention as usual, and get me sorted and connected with the in-crowd at school. Unfortunately not, this was just around the time that Ronan, my parents and teachers were finally after years of trying, about to give up on Ronan's public schooling. At this time, I remember he used to be getting extra classes at home and school trying to get him to the level that others in his class were at and he was finding it difficult even with all his work and his wish to stay there where he thought he should be. This obviously would make any young boy angry and confused as it did Ronan. His frustration would come out sometimes, and was only made worse when occasionally, children being children, were cruel to him at school. My recollection isn't the best, but I don't think he finished the year in the school.

Back at home after school, he'd always be up to mischief, tickling me silly if I got too close and hadn't remembered that he did exactly the same the day before and would again if given half a chance the next. He repetitively listened to Elvis, Jerry Lee Lewis, Tina friggin Turner and other such music from a by gone era, smart comment in hand for anything different about you today such as a new haircut, shirt or mismatching socks. He's always been the comedian of the family, the first to give you a difficult but fun time if you gave him half an opportunity or moment. This in comparison to the rest of us in the family who love to laugh also, but are usually too serious thinking about getting something done the rest of the time to be in that frame of mind. So, Ronan's input into anything he puts his time and effort into is always in good humour. And this is who he was after I received a brain injury in the summer of 2013.

This is when I was knocked out (concussion) for an unknown amount of time, but probably between 2 and 10 minutes. I remember waking in the Sikorsky helicopter, and like a little child wanting to get out of the patient seat and take photos with my phone, especially when I was told it was the new higher spec model just got by the coast guard that I had just been reading about previously. My next memory is standing across the road from the hospital, outside the shop on the corner, in backless lingerie they give patients at hospitals, opening a fresh box of cigarettes some kind soul bought me and calling home on their borrowed phone. I remember asking why I was over in Inisheer as I leaned against a traffic light pole in a considerably busier intersection in Limerick city than could be found anywhere on Inisheer, when my mother answered telling me she just got a phone from the hospital and that I had escaped again, with me having no recollection of escaping the first time and telling me to go back. But after a good 10 minutes on the call realising that I was in Limerick most likely and not on the little island of Inisheer made sense and decided I probably should go back. For the rest of my time in the Limerick hospital one security guard was on my door and the other at the door of my ward, just in case I tried to make a run again. Which I did of course, except that time I got confused trying to leave the building and didn't make the front door before being escorted back to my bed. So that was my first two days with a brain injury, similar to what Ronan has experienced for over 30 years. And I find myself wondering, how does he do it?

About three months later I was escaping Galway university hospital on the last of my routine weekend check-ups, when I was called back by one of the nurses who was adamant that I had to wait for the neurologist to speak to me before my permanent freedom from hospital check-ups and being treated like a guinea pig for 3 months. After impatiently waiting 30-40 minutes, and what felt considerably longer, the neurologist finally arrived and gave me a spiel about more than likely I'd be fine in three to six months but that there was a slight chance that it would take longer, like nine months or even up to 4years. Which I laughed at and ran out the door as I was only concerned about being 100% then and there, free. Or so I thought. During this time, I was at the start of repeating 2nd year of college due to missing the summer sitting of my exams because of the bang. More than 3 months after said bang, I was convinced everything would be as easy as it was the first time. As I began my repeat year, I had yet to learn.

As the college year progressed it was one kick after another, one failure after another, but I hadn't given up. Not even when I had been studying flat out for every available minute during a week for a law exam. My housemate who was in the same course turned to me one day and asked why I had spent the last 18 hours studying just the one same chapter that I had been studying for the last number of days. I thought I was studying the full subject and come to be told I had just been reading the same 12 pages for nearly a full day! I had no recollection of having finished the chapter once, never mind continuously for a number of days. Around the same time, I got lost in Galway city going from the docks to the city centre, which is a 5-10 minute walking journey that I have done thousands of time since childhood. All I had to do was cross two or three parallel streets and I was there. But as soon as I got off Dock Street onto Merchants Road and having what I would later name one of my "shiny moments", I looked up and I was lost, with no idea of where I had come from or even know what city I was in. Ten minutes later the joy and relief felt after realizing where I was, but then there was the question which I would get very used too very slowly, why was I there and what was I supposed to be doing there anyhow?

This would be a recurring theme over the next while and I still had my second semester of my repeat year to do. That was when the biggest kick came from my college repeat year, the macroeconomics exam. Something I had been reading in the tabloids and broadsheets since young adulthood and something I enjoyed immensely and had no problem passing even as in the previous years. This one was different and unlike all the previous ones that I had failed this year, I couldn't take it anymore, not macro. So, 1.5 hours into 2-hour macro exam, I left broken hearted. I could not answer a single question coherently or was getting a

71

total blank on every other question I knew that I knew. I just couldn't access that information. I had to get out of dodge. That was the moment of final realization hitting bottom, knowing I wasn't of the same ability that I thought or believed in until then. I walked out of college and wouldn't even pass through the grounds for another number of years again because of that day's memory. That was twelve months almost to the day after when I finally acknowledged the new truth of my situation.

Shortly after I was in a brain injury school taking (and failing miserably) an IQ test while being asked one or two questions. This was a test to see if it was an ABI (aggravated brain injury) or not and a test of my concentration ability. It was more than twelve months after the incident and the school was Quest in Galway. I'd get to know it quite well. But it was at this time that Ronan's influence would begin to influence my life a bit more again, as I had now pretty much finished at college he had turned around to me and told me that he too was a previous client of Quest and as I was starting there, the staff told me the same thing and a few of them were still there from his time. In doing brain train exercises and spending almost two years to update my CV, it was difficult not to remember my earlier childhood and those same training educational exercises we used to do with Ronan, and his anger as well at his inability to be able to do the desired task and not for lack of effort either. It was a flashback to those days in the boy's school again and a better understanding of Ronan's anger during those times.

So here I was with my head up my own arse for a good year fretting about my inability to do the shop if there was more than 3 items to get which would have to be continuously repeated during the walk to said shop with my head staring only at the pavement below because if I looked up in a crowded street and caught someone's eye it was another guaranteed "shiny moment" and everything in my head before that moment was gone, the list included and anything else in my head before of any consequence or need. Now the walk back home to try to remember the list again over the next hour, then try the excursion again and this time make sure not have anymore moments and head down in the ground and look at no one. Now I could understand much better Ronan's displeasure during those years when the hope was still that he could stay in the public school system, where he thought he should be and wanted to be at that time and maybe he may have sensed a similar situation with myself as well after my failed attempt at 3rd level and the effort involved.

So, he started cracking jokes about the 2 fools in the family, dumb and dumber as he liked to call us. I don't think I remember anyone being brave enough in the first year to try to make me laugh at all and even more so laugh about my current difficulties. But here was Ronan, king of the one-liners throwing in one barb after another continuously joking of the situation when absolutely no one else would dare too. Fair friggin play. Over the next year, Ronan would be in the car often as we two plebs would attempt to do the shopping using a note app on the phone but there would always be one more thing added as we would be walking out the door to the car, which every time we would never add to the list because we wanted to remember ourselves. Except Ronan would be joking about how we will forget before we even got out the gate of the house and sure enough some shiny moment of distraction would be guaranteed to happen before the shop and we'd both be sitting in the car park of the shop looking at the list on the phone laughing. Again, it was joking like that about the situation that gives people like ourselves a bit more acceptance to their circumstances, but no one had dared to joke about that, except Ronan to me, and I don't think anyone did for another year or two after either.

My acceptance came with the help of my brother and his jokes especially around the time of Quest and its brain training methodology and flashbacks of his youth and his non-acceptance of his situation around that time. That, after the abject failure of college, was difficult but here was king of the one-liners sitting in the passenger seat of the car with his head ever so slightly bopping out of the corner of my eye to the rhythm of my dance music playing and him throwing barbs and bringing up more original thought provoking conversation than most without even trying, just curiously wondering something and being comfortable enough in asking. Again, very hard to stay up your own ass, oh-woe-is-me mood next to that, and again fair-friggin play. Better man than I. ~*Donal*

Cliodhna's Story

I was born in 1983 into a beautiful loving family. My family consisted of my mother Agnes, my father Bertie and my three older brothers Rory, Ronan and Donal. I was the only girl and the apple of my father's eyes. I grew up as any other girl did with three older brothers. I learned how to fend for myself in sibling battles at a very early age (and won more than I lost). I never knew life any differently, and Ronan's accident and the extremely difficult journey of my family through the accident preceding my existence never affected my upbringing or the abundance of love that I felt in my family life.

Normal to me was arriving home from Naoinra at Collaiste Chonnacht in Coilleach, to all the Angel ladies (Nancy, Rose, Peggy, Caitriona) and my mother doing physio with Ronan on the kitchen table on a daily basis. Normal to me was seeing Sr. Dela, who was a special educational teacher in Spiddal, teaching Ronan in my school when I was in First Class. Normal to me was making the journey with my mother in the car from Spiddal into Galway to pick up my brother from the Holy Family School. And it was normal for me to pick up Ronan with my dad from Merlin Park where he went with other teenagers to learn life skills like cooking and cleaning amongst other daily activities.

Nobody ever made me feel that Ronan was ever 'disabled' as such. He had more life in him and more passion than a lot of 'abled' people I have met in my life to date. He is kind, he is funny and generous and extremely quick witted! He has a curiosity for life that I have rarely seen in most people I've met in mine. He is fascinated with technology and was one of the first people I knew in the 1990's to have a PC. His first computer was the Amstrad 464 and he was obsessed with it and had a passion for learning how to use technology, and this was before the internet ever existed. He has always been ahead of the trend when it came to technology and even to this day it amazes me how forward thinking he was at the time.

He loves music and has the memory of an elephant! His long-term memory is ferocious, and he can name a song and tell me the year quicker than I ever could within seconds of hearing the melody. His love and passion for music and travel has created life experiences for both him and my mother that is so inspirational to me. He has never been 'disabled' in life, and certainly not in his mind anyway, and as far as I am concerned, he is the most able-minded and strong-willed person I have ever encountered. He's extremely intelligent and perceptive with emotions and what is going on around him.

Another of Ronan's attributes that truly inspires me is his love for the world around him and his passion for traveling. This passion roped my mother into traveling further from home than she ever thought imaginable in her life. They have travelled all over the world together, from Graceland (stemming from his love for Elvis) to Australia, Hong Kong, Singapore, New York and more. Because of Ronan's thirst for traveling, my mother has taken it upon herself to make sure he sees the world, which he loves so much, a credit to her loving nature.

2005, Age 30, Ronan and Cliodhna in New York

Ronan has also influenced my life in a profound way. It is
only upon reflection that I realize its true impact. I have always
heard Ronan's voice in the back of my head telling me to go and
travel as I am more "free" to roam the corners of this earth with
whomever I please and whenever I please. It is for this reason I
have always said yes to everything adventurous, yes to a new
destination and yes to new challenges in life as I do not have such
physical barriers as Ronan.

I also went back to college in my 30's as another homage to
my brother's learning barriers. Although this commitment is
obviously for my benefit, I consider myself living my life as how
Ronan would have, had he never been dealt his set of cards. It is
also on this basis that I choose to seize each day with such passion
and joy as I realize with every breath in my body how lucky I am to
have certain experiences and Ronan cannot.

Ronan has never resented any of us, his siblings, for living
our own lives and experiencing our own adventures and this is a
testament to his character as well as all the others I have mentioned.

I hope this journey of writing this book with his dear friend Connor Meehan will show those of you reading it how he has lived through such adversity and become the stronger person because of it. As his youngest sibling and only sister, I would like to mention that Ronan shows more resilience in the face of hardship with such grace, pride, laughter and love than any person I have ever met. I have always been proud of him and so blessed that he is my brother. ~ *Cliodhna*

I hope these personal and heartfelt stories give the insights that I had hoped for. I'm more than grateful to my family for taking the time to write out their experiences. I know from my own experience that digging up memories and writing about them can be mixed. It can bring great clarity and joy, but it also has the very real potential of bringing up painful memories, which can hurt.

Chapter 10

"The world is a book, and those who do not travel read only one page."

~ Saint Augustine

My siblings brought up my love of travel which I have not mentioned much about. Travel has always been one of my passions. One of the trips I remember was going to Lourdes, France. I was 6 when we went to Lourdes as part of a church group to be part of the community and have a vacation from all the medical treatments. Bishop Eamon Casey joined us on the trip, and we traveled with many families. My family stayed in the hotel and I stayed in the hospital with many other kids not far from the basilica. We had great fun touring the city on a coach and there was singing and laughing.

1981 age 6, Ronan, Aunt Nessa, Maoilín, Maureen

Not long after that, we travelled to Malaga, Spain for holiday. We stayed a week in an apartment with a pool. One day, after watching my brother Rory diving into the pool, I decided I wanted to dive in as well, even though I was strapped into my wheelchair. With the weight of wheelchair, I sank to the bottom like a stone. At the time, my body was still twisted from the accident, and my arms and legs would have spasms, so I was well strapped into the wheelchair. Neither my mom or dad knew how to swim, but a lady from Dublin that were at the pool dove in before the lifeguards and hauled me and my wheelchair to the surface. I imagine that my mom and dad had a heart attack, but once out of the pool, I laughed and laughed.

1985, age 10. A family trip to Dingle. Donal, Cliodhna and Ronan

In my early twenties I travelled to America to go to visit Graceland, the home of my idol Elvis Presley. At this time in my recovery, I was having a very difficult time, and my mother, in an attempt to get me to take my medication, promised to take me to see Elvis if I would take my pills. She made this promise before even knowing where Graceland was. That morning at church, she saw an advertisement for Graceland and got the paper to try to figure out where Graceland was. There was a tour leaving from England that flew from Dublin, Ireland to Gatwick airport in London, England to join the tour group. All the tour guides had big beehive wigs, long nails and dressed like Elvis. It was the year of the OJ Simpson white Broncho chase. I was brought up to see the pilot before the plane left, and then we flew to Nashville, TN. The whole flight had Elvis music and everything. We saw Dolly Partons house and went on the General Jackson Steamboat on the Cumberland River and listened to the jazz music and ate barbeque. I remember going to the Grand Old Opre – I was so excited. George Hamilton V was on stage. It took so much energy to get into the building and to my seats, that I ended up sleeping through the whole performance. We took the Greyhound bus to Graceland. At the time, we were not allowed upstairs because Michael Jackson and Lisa Marie were staying there that night. I had a whole pocket full of spending money, but I wouldn't spend a dime because I wanted to save up to buy some of Elvis's jewellery. We went to the Hard Rock Café and to see the ducks at the Peabody hotel. As amazing as this was, it was not my all-time favourite trip.

1996, Age 21 Grand Ole Opry, Nashville Tennessee

1996, Age 21 Memphis

In 1997 we went to Blackpool, England for an Elvis Presley convention for the 20th anniversary of his death. I travelled with my mom, sister Cliodhna and brother Donal. Cliodhna (13) and Donal (15) agreed to go on the condition that we went to the theme park at least one day. We stayed at a bed and breakfast that was decorated from floor to ceiling with Elvis's. Not far from where we were staying, Granada studios was located where Coronation Street is filmed. There were shows and music, and the fella who was running the convention was from Galway.

In June 2004 we travelled to New York for 3 days and then onto Minnesota to visit my first nephew who was just 2 months old. We went to the site of the twin towers and we were meant to go to see Mama Mia, but our flight out of Shannon Ireland was delayed. I remember it was so busy. My mom and sister wanted to shop, and they kept leaving me in a café for "30 minutes" while they ran off to the shops. I'd say it was usually more than 30 minutes!

2005, Age 30, Ronan and Cliodhna in New York

In 2016 I went to Las Vegas with my mom, sister, brother Rory, his wife and her parents. It was a nice place and I'd like to go there again. We were mean to take a helicopter out to the Grand Canyon, but they couldn't fly that morning due to the clouds. We went to see an Elvis show and he was really good! I went to see David Copperfield with my sister-in-law's father Gene. We had front row seats and that show was my favourite part of the trip!

In 2018, I travelled to Iceland with my family. We went to see the geysers which have boiling hot water. They even had heated sidewalks outside the hotel because they use the ground water to heat them. We went to see the waterfalls which was my favourite part.

2018, age 43 Iceland

2018 was also one of my several trips back to Minneapolis, MN to visit my brother Rory and his family. In that particular year, we were in Minneapolis for the annual St. Patrick's Day parade.

2018, Ronan and Gene

Once again, this is a place where my story could reasonably end, but I would like to let you know about my life as it is today.

Chapter 11

"You can always chase a dream, but it will not count if you never catch it."

~ Malcom X

I would like in this final chapter to give a brief insight of my life as it is today. I'll describe my morning yesterday in an honest effort to show how things that everyone takes for granted and rightfully so, can be an issue for me. There is no part of me that writes about this with self-pity or defeatism, my intention here is to give a real indication of a representative daily activity that requires more effort than might otherwise be the case.

I like to get up early, it has always been my way and one of the things that I like in the morning is hot toast with real butter melting onto it. I got up yesterday at a normal time, but by the time I was able to make my tea, my toast had gone cold. I am not able to do this seemingly mundane and everyday task quickly enough to enjoy the warm toast that I like so much. My mother with her mother's intuition and love, once again, came to my rescue and helped me.

My mother and I live in her home village in the western end of our island, and we live in harmony to a great degree with the normal ups and downs that go along with family life.

We drive to Kilronan most days, either to the shops or to work, or to stop in Kilmurvey where my Aunts have a café, Teach Nan Phaidi, and another Aunt has a shop. Elvis likes to ride in the car with us, and our journey is usually slow if we are stuck behind a jaunty car, or tourists on bicycles, but I don't mind so much.

2018, In Kilmurvey outside the shops and the café

2018, Our home in Onacht

2018, Our view to the sea

I have struggled historically during the winter time as my work finishes, and I have to be very vigilant to keep as active and busy as I possibly can as this is the best antidote that was ever known to combat stinking thinking – which I am not immune from.

There has been a dramatic change in my life over the last 2 or 3 years in that I have wanted to write and express myself for years. A couple of years ago, I started writing a blog which was read by people from all over the world. I would like very much to put in this book, a selection of my favourite blogs from the last couple of years. I hope they manage to give some sort of insight as to my life as a disabled man and how I have tried to acknowledge my limitations but never allowed them to become barriers.

Having people from all over the world read my blogs made me feel great and explicitly encouraged me to continue chasing my dream. All the time, while I was writing my blog, I had this thought in the back of my mind that I really wanted to write my own story.

When I was writing the blogs, I dreamt of writing a book. Now that this book is coming to an end, I am dreaming and planning to write more books and poems. The writing has changed my life and brought a purpose that I was craving all my life. I have included the blog posts below for your enjoyment.

I read once that "anything is possible". This disabled island man believes this now, and if I was in a form of prison before, I can now see the light streaming in the windows and the door beginning to open for me. My story naturally concludes at this point, and if you enjoyed it, even a fraction of the amount that I've enjoyed it, then I couldn't feel happier. I said at the outset that I was hoping above anything else, that the telling of my story may help others. This will be for others to judge but if this story has managed to help or encourage anyone, well, then my work is done.

I hope you reading my story as much as I have enjoyed writing it!

Blog Posts

https://www.facebook.com/AranIslands/

January 21, 2018

ARAN ISLANDS.

A Winter with a difference.

Good Afternoon.

I am very keen to keep in touch with you readers - primarily as you have all enriched and changed my life for the better.

Winter has historically been a challenging and tricky time for me but this winter for the first time ever, it has been different and better.

The reason for this is ; I have the happy task of writing my book which is essentially my life story.
Even though it has brought up some stuff that I had buried, it has brought purpose, vitality and energy to my life and I feel that now that I am on this journey, I will never go back to how it was before.

Thanks to each and every one of you, for your support and encouragement.

Rònàn Faherty.

Dec 3, 2017

ARAN ISLANDS.

Great to be Home.

Good Afternoon,

I spent the last 3 weeks in Merlin Park Hospital and firstly I can only say good and positive things about the care that I received there.

There is an old saying that says - every savage loves his native shore--- well, I feel so so happy and grateful to be finally at home on my native Island.

There were long dark nights in the hospital when my initial thoughts were to give up on writing my book and pull the covers up over my head, but I remembered how we are not responsible for the first thought that comes into our heads, but we are responsible for the second thought.

With this in mind I decided to sit with the fear and uncertainty and think things through.
Like Charles Darwin said about the animal kingdom - it's the animals most open to and adaptable to change that survive best --- I thought things through and realised that writing my book is not just hugely important to me, it also puts incredible meaning and purpose in my life.

I looked into a black space but the outcomes for me were really positive and powerful.
I am more determined now than ever in writing my book and even though I may be wrong, I have a strong feeling inside that my story may help others.

Thanks to you all for supporting and encouraging me.

Rònàn Faherty.

Nov 16, 2017

ARAN ISLANDS

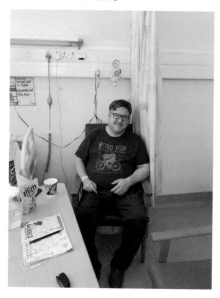

Oct 22, 2017

ARAN ISLANDS

Island Life and Book Update.

Good Afternoon,

As most of you will probably know by now - I have started writing a book which is essentially my life story. It may appear initially to be the story of a disabled man from and living on an Island, but I hope in my heart of hearts, that it is truly much more than that. My story is the only one that I can tell and to be honest, I have been very reluctant to write it- for a variety of reasons.

A change occurred and a thought came to my mind "what if my story ends up helping, encouraging or even inspiring someone, be they disabled or not - then I feel it is more than worth it to write my story, even though I find it painful at times ".

The advice we received was to write 3 chapters and a synopsis and bring that much to prospective publishers and take it from there.

Well, the 3 chapters are done, and I sincerely hope it's ok to ask this but would anyone out there be able to help me by getting some introductions to prospective publishers.

I hope it's ok to ask this and any help would mean the world to me.

Thank you.

I like to finish with a quote, "it's not knowing what to do, it's doing what you know"
Anthony Robinson.

I will keep in touch and thank you so much for reading.

Rònàn Faherty.

(Left) Rory, (Right) Correna with Dado

(Left) Donal, (Middle) Orla, (Right) Ronan

(Left) Mamo, (Right) Dado (my mom's parents)

Sept 22, 2017

ARAN ISLANDS

My Book Begins,

Good Morning,

I'd just like to give the briefest of updates and stay in touch with you all.

When I finished my work up at Dùn Aonghusa, I started writing a book. It is essentially my own life story.
It's certainly easier to write about anything except yourself.
I am really finding this process to be very rewarding even though it can also be painful at times.

I'll stay in touch and thanks.

Rònàn Faherty.

(Left) Ronan, (Right) Oisin

Ronan at Teach Nan Phaidi's

Aug 25, 2017

ARAN ISLANDS.

SUMMERTIME COMING TO AN END, BUT WINTERTIME NOW FEELS DIFFERENT TO ME.

Good Afternoon,

I'm firstly hoping that everyone has had a good and enjoyable summer.

This time of year there are many, many changes occurring on my Island home - some are subtle and some are not, but all are beautiful.

At this time of year, historically I finish my work up at Dùn Aonghusa and I find myself facing unemployment and wintertime. I have often struggled with both in different ways.

This year as the end of the summer approaches, there is an occurrence that is making a significant difference in my views and to the quality of my life.

That difference is; that I am going to write a book this winter, which will be my own life story.

I have been blessed with a great life to date but being a disabled man on an island has brought up some challenges but I'd like to think that, to date - I've been equal to them.

I know in some ways that writing my book, it will be challenging but overall , I feel very positive and happy at the prospect of writing my story.

In advance, I would like to thank you all for your support and encouragement and I would not be stretching it by saying that without this blog and all of you readers - this book would never happen.

I will continue to blog but possibly a little more infrequently due to the book but please know how important your readership, support and encouragement is to me.

I'll finish with a quote
" even if you're on the right track, you'll get run over if you just sit there ".
Will Rogers.

Rònàn Faherty.

Aug 18, 2017

ARAN ISLANDS

CHANGE

Good Afternoon,

I think every human being has the challenge in their lives in dealing with change.
The goal is to not just anticipate it but to embrace it.
I usually find myself fearful of change and reluctant to consider change. Yet, my own life experiences clearly shows me that there is nothing to actually be fearful of.
It's just a piece of human nature or maybe cultural programming, but either way - I feel very determined to embrace change and to try and enjoy it instead of being afraid of it.

For the last few months, I have been working up at Dùn Aonghusa and I really enjoy going to do my work and one of the many positive and happy routines that has evolved in my life is ; when I finish work, I go for something to eat.
This simple routine that so many may take for granted makes me feel great and to be honest , I am fearful, reluctant and definitely not looking forward to that changing and ending.

While I have so much in my life to be grateful for and I genuinely don't like to sound ungrateful - I find myself kinda dreading the thoughts of my work ending and going back to being unemployed.

This winter I firmly resolve to stay positive and to be as productive and useful to my community as I can possibly be.

I had planned to have my first swim of this year with a friend of mine, but the inclement weather dictated otherwise. I will most definitely do it soon and will attempt to describe it to you all.

I'll finish off with a quote
" failure is the condiment that gives success its flavour "
Truman Capote.

Rònàn Faherty.

Aug 11, 2017

ARAN ISLANDS.

Island Wedding.

Good Afternoon,

I was delighted to be asked to the wedding of my first cousin, Fainche who got married to a very fine fellow called, Jason here on this island.

While first, second and third thoughts are just to wish them every happiness and health in their life together, it also struck me as I sat there with my brothers ;

A lot of people come from the mainland to get married here, A lot from here go to the mainland to get married so it was extra special to see someone from here getting married here - and to make it even better, they came back from Perth to get married at home.

I also looked at their love and happiness and while I wished nothing but good from the bottom of my heart - I couldn't help but wonder if I'll ever know such love in my own life.

I didn't join the others on the dance floor, and I can't be 100% sure whether it's my disability or just that I'm not a dancer but either way, I happily remained in the safety and security of my own seat!!!

Finally, I would like to give a big shout out to one the biggest supporters and friends of this blog and of myself---
Vivienne Nichols and her husband David, are on inis meain for a month again this year and as Vivienne had major surgery during the winter --- things were touch and go for her during the winter back home in Tennessee - this trip is more than a small bit meaningful to her and to us.

I'll finish with a quote
" dreams come a size too big, so we can grow into them ".
Josie Bissett.

Rònàn Faherty.

(Left) Rory, (Middle) Donal, (Right) Ronan

Aug 4, 2017

ARAN ISLANDS

Access to Dùn Aonghusa.

Good Afternoon,

I am aware that I am in a very small minority as I write, but writing this piece is hugely passionate to me and very important to those who need a voice.

I don't assume to be anyone's voice or advocate but as I was up at Dùn Aonghusa at my work today, I was kinda surprised at how every single time I go up there; I am deeply impacted and moved by its beauty and grandeur.

This got me thinking ; and as a disabled man, my thoughts went to those who can't access this magical and beautiful place - it's because of how it makes me feel that I find myself compelled to seek better disabled access as there is not only beauty there , but in this humble island man's opinion - healing to be found up there too.

I hope especially that more people with mobility issues can get this unique experience.

I'll finish with a quote
"It's impossible to please all the world and one's father ".

Rònàn Faherty.

July 28, 2017

ARAN ISLANDS

My Brother Rory and his wife's return.

Good Afternoon,

There is a great and happy feeling of anticipation in this household and in my heart in particular.
The reason for this is that my older brother, Rory and wife, Kari are coming home to visit tomorrow.
When I see the boat pulling in with Rory on board my heart soars and beats out of my chest with the happiness of seeing my brother coming home to our Island.
Because I will be starting to write a book in September which is essentially the story of my life - I find myself thinking a bit about

the path my life has taken and part of this process has been looking at the different paths that my life and Rory's lives have taken.

On some levels, I think my accident determined and dictated my own path but to be honest - accident or no accident, I believe our paths would have always been destined to be different , while all the time sharing the unbreakable bond of being brothers.

I will finish with a quote of my own if that's ok ---
" you don't have to be brain damaged to be forgetful, everyone can be forgetful "

Rònàn Faherty.

July 21, 2017

ARAN ISLANDS

A LIFE AT SEA, PAST & PRESENT.

Good Afternoon,

I feel very connected to the fishing industry as my family have been fishing for generations and indeed, some still are.

I know that fishing is a way of life rather than just a job.
I have seen at first hand all my life how going to sea to fish is a very primal activity and when I see the passion in those brave souls , I must confess to a little jealously - having such deep and abiding passion is really admirable and desirable.

I have thought and wondered over the years ;

If I didn't have my accident all those years ago , would I have harvested the sea like my people before and been a fisherman. I can never honestly answer that question but --- hey, it's ok to dream !!

I'll finish with a quote please ---
" the education of a man is never completed until he dies "
Robert E Lee.

Rònàn Faherty.

July 8, 2017
ARAN ISLANDS.

SAILING BOATS VISIT MY ISLAND HOME.

Good Afternoon,

For many many years this Island was visited by Sailing Boats - in the past these were working Sailing Boats that were essentially cargo boats, coming here from Connemara with turf as we have no boglands here and very often leaving with fish in exchange. These brave men provided an invaluable service to my forefathers and the boats and the boatmen were always so welcome.

The visiting sailing boats that are here just now, may be here for sport but they are every bit as welcome as those much loved connemara turf boats.

Looking out at all the boats and witnessing the wonderful atmosphere that they have created on my Island Home, I feel that it would be great if there was more of this here as we are surrounded by great sailing waters and I'd like to think that we offer a warm welcome along with the uniqueness of this Island location. These sailors are a great boost and are heartily welcome.

I'll finish with a quote
" don't worry about failures, worry about the chances you miss when you don't even try "
Jack Canfield.

Rònàn Faherty.

June 30, 2017 ·

ARAN ISLANDS

Working up at Dùn Aonghusa.

Good Afternoon,

Today is the last day of June and sun is shining brightly on my Island home.

I often mentioned in the depths of winter how I miss work, value working and would love to be going to work.

I feel it's only right that I mention that as it's summer , I am working up at Dùn Aonghusa - all the things that I mentioned about the dignity of working and feeling useful in myself, partly because I am working away - are very true and today I am grateful to have all the positive feelings and associations from doing my work.

I am no different to anyone else in that I'm sure I could root out a few negatives but I'm not inclined to - my memory is fresh and so is my awareness.

I'm mindful of an old proverb ;
" you never miss the water until the well runs dry ".

Rònàn Faherty.

June 23, 2017
ARAN ISLANDS.

THOUGHTS ON RED BULL CLIFF DIVING.

There is a palpable feeling of excitement with the Red Bull Cliff Diving Championship being held in my island home.

Poll na bPeist as we call it out here has been a favourite place of my family for generations and I am so happy see the cliff diving organisers picking such a spectacular and dramatic location for the diving.

Like a lot of beautiful places, it's greatest beauty lies in the fact that this unique and special place is all Mother Nature's work.
Imagine - a perfectly rectangular pool carved out by nature in this stunning location.

I feel quietly proud that the world is able to see this place in it's raw and untamed beauty.

I'd like to commend and praise the organisers for picking this unique place and for doing such a wonderful job.

If there was one criticism, I would like to make the point - as a disabled man and on behalf of all people with disabilities, that while I more than understand that picking a remote and beautiful place has many many positives - access for people like myself is not great and I know that lots of people in my position would love the chance to see it live.

I feel bad mentioning a negative but feel compelled to advocate on behalf of my fellow people with disabilities.

Very well done to the organisers on an excellent job though.

Finally, a quote
"When the best things are not possible, the best may be made of those that are".

Rònàn Faherty.

June 16, 2017 ·

ARAN ISLANDS.

Realizations on the benefits of being back at work.

Good Afternoon,

I was in work up at Dùn Aonghusa yesterday and when i saw a cruise ship passing by from my cliff top vantage point, i immediately took a picture on my phone.

After i took the picture, i was aware that there was a definite lack of some of my previous feelings in that ; i didnt wish i was on that ship and felt more than happy to be exactly where i was.
There were a number of reasons for this

A) i am working and feel good about that.

B) writing this blog and connecting with the outside world feels great.

C) i feel good in myself.

Before i set off to walk home after work , i saw people doing Tai Chi and also saw people setting up for the Red Bull Diving Championships that is on here next week - i loved seeing these sights and in addition to that, while i was walking home, i saw a Robin with a snail in his beak - now, i am sure there are many many things that i dont know but i know for sure that i wouldnt see or experience any of the above from under the duvet.

I'll finish with a quote
" laugh and the world laughs with you, snore and you sleep alone"
Anthony Burgess.

Rònàn Faherty.

June 9, 2017 ·

ARAN ISLANDS.

ISLAND LIFE.

Good Evening,

My thoughts this evening are with a neighbour of mine who was taken to hospital in Galway via lifeboat from this Island.

I ended up in casualty this week myself but was fortunate to be able to take the ferry out and most importantly - i had the help and support of my mother.
My trip to casualty was routine enough and was a result of me falling - not my first time and more than likely , wont be my last one !!!

The first picture above is of me as a child when i used to be in a wheelchair. Thankfully, i no longer need to use the wheel chair but i am reminded , by my neighbour, of two recent trips i had to hospital in Galway.
One was by lifeboat, the other by helicopter - and injuries aside , i loved being on the boat at sea and am aware at all times how on a good or normal day a journey from my island home always starts by crossing the ocean by ferry or plane but sometimes through

illness or injury, the journey can be made by helicopter or lifeboat and instead of the bus in to town - an ambulance is the mode of transport.

Driving fast towards the hospital with the sirens going and driving through red lights is a form of excitment but it also brings home to me how there is always an extra dimension to living on an island. Generally, the extra dimension of island life is good and positive but hardships are part of our life out here and in truth , they are best accepted.

Finally a quote of my own
" in the act of humanity, we wish to be free to do what we want to do "

Rònàn Faherty.

May 17, 2017 ·

ARAN ISLANDS

My Dog, Friend & Companion ; Elvis.

Good Afternoon,

As i spend more time with my dog , Elvis, than anyone else, i found myself writing a poem about him.

It made me think about the importance and value of my relationship with my dog, Elvis. I initially thought only pet owners might get this fully, but i know when i went over to America to see my brother, Rory (pictured) and his wonderful family at Christmas - more than pet owners identified with how much i missed Elvis and how i was thrilled to see him when i got home.

For sure, i missed my island home, but for now - i will just mention Elvis and return to how much i missed home again - i was so comfortable and happy to return home but my joy at seeing Elvis impacted massively.

I am going back to work up at Dùn Aonghusa in a couple of weeks for the OPW, and im so looking forward to that.

I love meeting the people and feel really proud to see them enjoying my island home so much.

I also love the structure and dicipline that it brings to my life - the wages dont hurt either !!!

I'll finish with a quote of my own if i may
" eat well, sleep good & work hard and you will live a good life"

Rònàn Faherty.

May 30, 2017 ·

ARAN ISLANDS.

My Thoughts on Vacant Buildings and Homelessness.

Good Afternoon,

I was sitting on the bench down at the old pier eating a 99 ice cream and it was impossible not to notice the vacant pierside buildings across the harbour from me.
It is a great pity that these fine waterside buildings are empty and i feel if they were developed that they could house fine businesses that would provide much needed jobs.

This got me thinking. It sure is a pity to see empty and vacant commercial buildings but it is a tragedy to see all the vacant houses on this island and further afield. My great sadness is for all the poor people who find themselves without a home and are living on the streets, in hotels , in bed and breakfasts or some such place that is definitely not their home.

My heart goes out to these poor people and even though it is a complex problem , part of the solution has got to be us all taking simple, decisive and positive action.

I will finish with a quote
" the first step to getting the things you want out of life, is to decide what it is you want"
Ben Stein.

Rònàn Faherty.

May 23, 2017 ·

ARAN ISLANDS.

Walking, Fresh Air and their benefits.

Good Afternoon,

Even though i like walking and talking pictures , it can sometimes be a bit of a challenge due to my disability.
I read during the week, that disability does not mean inability. That principal is very close to my heart and the fact that it can be difficult to walk somedays, to cross rough ground to get the photo that i want and if im honest there is quite a long list of reasons and what often appear as barriers are actually not - i am certainly not a saint or indeed an example of anything but today, i am especially appealling to those people with any form of disability or difficulty - not to give up, to please push through and to keep going.

I have discovered that most of us can actually do more than we think and the pure satisfaction of getting out of our comfort zone is more than worth it.

Fear stops and stunts so many of us but my life is enriched on a daily basis by that extra push. If one person draws encouragement from this, i will go to sleep tonight as a happy man.

I will finish with a quote

" in 3 words i can sum up everything ive learned about life ; it goes on ".

By Robert Frost.

Rònàn Faherty.

May 17, 2017 ·

ARAN ISLANDS

My Dog, Friend & Companion ; Elvis.

Good Afternoon,

As i spend more time with my dog , Elvis, than anyone else, i found myself writing a poem about him.

It made me think about the importance and value of my relationship with my dog, Elvis. I initially thought only pet owners might get this fully, but i know when i went over to America to see my brother, Rory (pictured) and his wonderful family at Christmas - more than pet owners identified with how much i missed Elvis and how i was thrilled to see him when i got home.

For sure, i missed my island home, but for now - i will just mention Elvis and return to how much i missed home again - i was so comfortable and happy to return home but my joy at seeing Elvis impacted massively.

I am going back to work up at Dùn Aonghusa in a couple of weeks for the OPW, and im so looking forward to that.
I love meeting the people and feel really proud to see them enjoying my island home so much.

I also love the structure and dicipline that it brings to my life - the wages dont hurt either !!!

I'll finish with a quote of my own if i may
" eat well, sleep good & work hard and you will live a good life"

Rònàn Faherty.

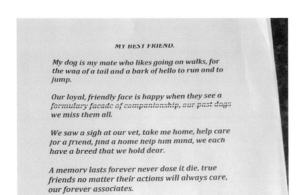

May 9, 2017 ·

ARAN ISLANDS

Thoughts and memories of the Darkness into Light Charity Walk.

Good Afternoon,

The Darkness into Light walk is held around Ireland (including here) every year , to raise money and awareness about suicide.

Last year, my sister Cliodhna did the walk and i was inspired when i saw how much it meant to her.

To be honest that was just a part of my own personal motivation for getting involved.

I had 2 friends who died through suicide and their tragic and untimely deaths impacted on me very deeply.

With the motivation of my sister, the memory of my friends and strength that i have found as a direct result of writing this blog - i was determined to do it this year for the first time.

It is a positive and healthy thing that suicide is being discussed openly and honestly and i feel priveleged to have been involved with this cause and while it may be too late for some , i sincerely hope that the next generation are not as burdened and always know there is someone willing to listen and share.

I saw the next generation last Sunday when my cousin's son made his first holy communion and it was a day that could only have been described as happy.

I'll finish with a quote
" i look on that man as happy, who, when there is question of success, looks into his work for a reply."
Ralph Emerson.

Rònàn Faherty.

Aran Islands

May 2, 2017 ·

ARAN ISLANDS

My Everest

Good Evening,

There is a very steep hill beside this house at the western end of my Island home , it is called Carcair an Robinson.

It is a very tough climb but you are rewarded the most beautiful views imaginable at the top.

I am aware that alot of people are fotunate and indeed, blessed enough to be able to just decide on a hike like this.

Fairly or unfairly, i am not one of these people.
My disability makes a climb like this very difficult and arduous but not impossible.

I dreamed about making it up the hill again and soaking that view that honestly makes my heart sing. I didnt feel it would happen or i would find the strength to face it but like everyone else i found the motivation.

I wanted with all my heart to challenge myself with two goals/dreams in mind ;
I wanted the simple satisfaction of standing up there, sweating and out of breath but happy.

I also, wanted to write about it and share this experience with the kind readers of my blog.
The encouragement that i have received has really motivated and fuelled me while filling my heart at the same time.

Thank you all for helping this Island man achieve and enjoy reaching this goal and dream that i have held.

I am hoping that this simple thank you does justice to the kindness that i have been shown.

Please enjoy the views.

I will finish with a quote of my own
" dream big, work hard and the rewards will be good "

Rònàn Faherty.

April 13, 2017 ·

ARAN ISLANDS.

LIAM O FLAHERTY, ISLAND AUTHOR.

Good Day,

I was asked recently to write a small piece about the great Island Author , Liam O'Flaherty --- a kind of a tribute and information. I was really pleased to be asked as ;

I think my simple blog has helped people see that even though i may have my own difficulties, i am thrilled to be able to write these humble pieces and find the support that i receive has changed my life so much - for the better.

Liam O Flaherty deserves every piece of praise he gets and more - as his writings have influenced and inspired so so many, including myself.

Liam O Flaherty is my great grand uncle and his influence has been immense in liturary circles but his direct influence on my family has brought nothing but pleasure.

Liam O Flaherty, particularlly in his short stories writes about the wonder and magic in nature and describes with an experiential sensitivity and insight the wonder and beauty of such simple Island occurrances as ; lambs being born and the spring digging of potatoe ridges.

He writes what it is like to have the conflicted feelings and emotions of the potatoe digger such as his desire to feed and protect his family along side his fear and self doubt - courageously human.

He somehow manages to be almost able to see things from the animals perpective - unique and beautiful.

I dont say this in any way lightly but i am very proud and honoured to be related to a man who was so gifted and rare.

A national treasure.

Rònàn Faherty.

My thoughts of Liam O'Flaherty.

Liam O'Flaherty was born on 28 August 1896 and died 7 September 1984, was an Irish novelist and short story O'Flaherty was born in the remote village of Gort na gCapall, his nephew Breandán Ó hEithir, he served as a staff journalist with (RTÉ), working on the current affairs programmes Cúrsaí and Féach.

Liam O'Flaherty was an Irish novelist and short story writer and a major figure in the Irish literary renaissance, O'Flaherty died on 7 September 1984, he is buried in Dublin, and many of his works were subsequently republished, he is remembered today as a powerful writer and a strong voice in Irish culture.

O'Flaherty was born, a son of Maidhc Ó Flaiherth and Maggie Ganley, at Gort na gCapall, at the age of twelve, he went to Rockwell Collage and later University College Dublin and the Dublin Diocesan teacher training college Holy Cross College, according to The Sunday Times, he also attended Belvedere College and Blackrock College.

It was intended he enter the priesthood, but in 1917 he joined the British Army as a member of the Irish Guards, in 1917 under the name 'Bill Ganly'. serving on the Western Front, he found trench life devastatingly monotonous but was badly injured in September 1917 during the Battle of Langemarck, it is speculated that the shell shock suffered was responsible for the mental illness which became apparent in 1933.

He returned from the front a socialist, having become interested in Marxism as a schoolboy, atheistic and communistic beliefs evolved in his 20s and he was a founder member of the Communist Party of Ireland, two days after the establishment of the Irish Free State, O'Flaherty and other unemployed Dublin workers seized the [then] Rotunda Concert Hall (later the Ambassador Cinema and now the Gate Theatre) in Dublin and held it for four days flying a red flag, in protest at "the apathy of the authorities". Free State troops forced their surrender.

April 4, 2017 ·

ARAN ISLANDS.

The Gap of Life.

Good Afternoon ,

I was out rambling earlier on and one of the little habits that i have devolped is, looking at the animals behaviors and the patterns of nature that is all around me.

I stood at the gate and was quietly looking at a field of cattle, and noticed that for what appeared to be no particular reason , one animal went through the gap in the wall leading from one field to next , and one by one , every single one of the cattle followed.
I have seen donkey's do that also.
Looking at that sight also made me think and realise that we humans also do a version of following one another through the various gaps too.

I dont have the answers really but i couldnt help thinking that life's real challenge and reward lies in ; being yourself and walking your own path through your own gaps.

Finally i would like to post a quote if i may
" people who cannot recognize a palpable absurdity are very much in the way of civilization ".
Agnes Repplier.

Rònàn Faherty.

March 28, 2017 ·

ARAN ISLANDS

Positive Island changes.

Good Afternoon ,

Two things happened during this week as i walked in my home village.

I walked past where the great Island poet , Màirtìn O Direàin , was born and raised and i paused to realise how much i admire his writings but also, how much i enjoy them too.

I walked past the church in onaght where my parents were married and where i was baptized - i also saw several pairs of pheasants who appeared to engaging in some sort of mating or courtship ritual , i also was happy to see the new born calves in the fields with their mom's and all of those little images on my island walk left me with a positive glow and feelings.

Finally, a quote of my own --
" live life as there is no tomorrow, and you live a full life ".

Rònàn Faherty.

March 21, 2017 ·

ARAN ISLANDS.

A Rare Snow Shower on My Island.

Good Day,

I headed out for a walk earlier on with my dog Elvis - to be honest, i was greatly encouraged by the readers of this blog who's support has helped me in my life in every way possible.

When i saw the snow shower, insticntively i said to myself - there is no way i should go out in that but i was fortunately able to cast my mind back and draw on the support i have. Walking may be a bit difficult but it is not impossible !

When i was walking and before the sun came back out, i was looking at the snow falling all around me and thought of an old Irish saying, which translates as
"What is seldom is wonderful " --- while alot of places in the world have snow as part of their daily lives, it is an occasional visitor here and it's white dusting is truly magical.

The snow disappeared but i enjoyed seeing it and enjoyed comparing it to many parts of life that can be ; fleeting, transient and beautiful.

Finally a quote if i may ;
" you can accomplish much if you dont care who gets the credit "
Ronald Reagan.

To all the readers, thanks very much for reading.

Rònàn Faherty.

March 8, 2017 ·

ARAN ISLANDS

The Difference in two Days.

Good Evening,

I was out walking today and saw the aftermath and consequences of all the recent rainfall.

It was stunning today and the warmth of the Spring sunshine was a sharpe contrast to yesterday's rain and fog.

It brought a number of thoughts to my mind ; firstly, was the dramatic difference in two day's weather, it's hard to believe two days can be so dramatically different.
I also thought about how in recent years, i often used the bad weather as an excuse not to go out - and felt slightly uncomfortable in myself when i realised a well known saying
" there is no such thing as bad weather - only bad clothes ".

I used to have a rainjacket that i got from Fàs (community employment scheme) , that i had from when i was lucky enough to work with them a few years ago and feel i need to replace it now.

It never ceases to amaze me at how every simple thing in life can be an opportunity to learn.

A quote of my own if i may

" believe you can, and you will always succeed ".

Rònàn Faherty.

March 1, 2017 ·

ARAN ISLANDS.

My Island Walk.

Good Evening,

I live back at the Western end of this Island and i am truly spoiled for choice when it comes to picking a route for my daily walk.

If im honest - my dog Elvis gets me out walking more than anything else.
Like alot of things, i had to go through a process in order to give myself permission to enjoy my daily Island walks.
I initially found it hard to accept that i couldnt run and my first response was to do absolutely nothing but this very quickly felt wrong.
From somewhere, i came slowly to the realisation that while my condition makes it impossible to run - i realised, that i can walk --- so i did and i do.

I always feel better for the bit of exercise and being out in the fresh air - and as i mentioned ; i get tremendous happiness and pleasure in seeing Elvis running free and enjoying himself.

No different to anyone else, i find myself with choices to make everyday and have learned what enhances my life and brings joy and quality of life - walking in the fresh air is right up there.

Id like to pop up a quote please ;
" desperate affairs require desperate remedies "
Horatio Nelson.

Thanks for reading.

Rònàn Faherty.

February 21, 2017 ·

ARAN ISLANDS

My Winter Poem.

Good Evening,

I am going to try and write what it was like to write the poem that i posted just now.

The first thing that i would like to do, is to thank every single one of you for reading my poem and for kindly allowing me to share my thoughts, hopes & fears with you all.

Normally i sit at my computer and i find myself looking at YouTube and the likes, primarily for music and documentaries which i really enjoy. Going into my room to write a poem or blog is an altogether different experience - firstly, it brings me out of my comfort zone which can be both exciting and a little scary but i have learned from my experience that i ultimately enjoy stretching myself emotionally and using my brain.

As i mentioned last time, this activity, which i love - definitely connects me to the outside world and takes the edge off my lonliness. I sit there and even though sometimes i cant write at all, i feel very grateful for the times that i can find the words. I didnt use the spellchecker on my computer but please enjoy my simple poem and the random pictures of my home Island.

I will finish with a quote of my own, if i may ;

" be yourself and not someone else. Because life is too short to be someone else ".

Thanks again, for reading.

Rònàn Faherty.

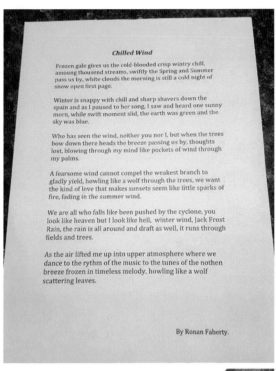

Chilled Wind

Frozen gale gives us the cold-blooded crisp wintry chill, amoung thousend streams, swiftly the Spring and Summer pass us by, white clouds the morning is still a cold night of snow open first page.

Winter is snappy with chill and sharp shavers down the spain and as I paused to her song, I saw and heard one sunny morn, while swift moment slid, the earth was green and the sky was blue.

Who has seen the wind, neither you nor I, but when the trees bow down there heads the breeze passing us by, thoughts lost, blowing through my mind like pockets of wind through my palms.

A fearsome wind cannot compel the weakest branch to gladly yield, howling like a wolf through the trees, we want the kind of love that makes sunsets seem like little sparks of fire, fading in the summer wind.

We are all who falls like been pushed by the cyclone, you look like heaven but I look like hell, winter wind, Jack Frost Rain, the rain is all around and draft as well, it runs through fields and trees.

As the air lifted me up into upper atmosphere where we dance to the rythm of the music to the tunes of the nothen breeze frozen in timeless melody, howling like a wolf scattering leaves.

By Ronan Faherty.

February 8, 2017 ·

ARAN ISLANDS.

Island Life.

Good Evening,

Its very mixed weather on my island home these days. It is strange in ways, how the weather
very often reflects the rythm of our lives and moods - or is it the other way around !!!

My day starts the same way every morning.
When i get up out of the bed, the first thing i do before i leave my room is ; i search for a meaningful quote and post it on my Facebook.
I dont believe in feeling sorry for myself in any way due to having a disability and am full of determination to play these cards, the very best way that i can.
I like going online with the quote as in some ways it kinda plugs me into the outside world.
At this stage , hunger is making itself known to me but before i fill my belly - my dog and friend, Elvis needs his brekkie and to run outside.
After that , i go into the kitchen - and i know i have made mention of having a disability and while it can honestly make some day to day tasks a bit more difficult - i decided many years ago that, i would never ever let it define me.
I am aware every day of my life that there are others who are worse off.

Living on my home Island with my family and in my community means the world to me. Finally, a quote
" the most profound joy has more of gravity than of gaiety in it ".

Rònàn Faherty.

February 1, 2017 ·

ARAN ISLANDS

Island of Beauty, Dreams and Realities.

Good Evening,

Like most things in life, my return to my Island home has been mixed.

Partly because it is home and partly because the raw and untamed beauty of my home island impacts on me in a way that really goes beyond any words i might have and it touches the tenderest parts of my heart and soul.

Alongside that, coming back to my life in the winter can be a challenge - i walked along the road with my dog and friend, Elvis - near Loch Chorruch and saw the machines and looked at the great work that the lads had done (it is photographed) . Without feeling sorry for myself, my heart kinda sank as my own reality of my disability limits the work i can actually do - it is difficult but not impossible.
If i was fully fit and able bodied, i know the opportunities for work would be much greater but my reality is ; i must accept the hand ive been dealt without lying down or giving up.
Every day and as long as my name is Rònàn , i will do every single thing in my power to not just find some sort of work but to go on with dignity.

I will finish with a quote of my own now, if that's ok ---

" there are no facts about the past or present - there are only truths "

Rònàn Faherty.

January 19, 2017 ·

ARAN ISLANDS

Thoughts & Memories of my trip to Las Vegas and Minneapolis.

Good Evening,

I left my Island home on 18th of Dec, we went to Chicago via Dublin and on to snowy Minneapolis for a few days before taking off for Las Vegas.

Las Vegas couldnt be more different from my home Island but i liked it very much. I went to The David Copperfield Magic Show and was really enjoyable.
Our plans had been to take a helicopter trip around the Grand Canyon but like we often experience at home , the weather had different plans for us that day - ill definitely try and do it again and hope there will be no fog to stop us !!!

My sister, Cliodhna, bungee jumped off the highest building in Las Vegas , it was really exciting watching her and i admired her courage and nerve , greatly.

I enjoyed shopping for clothes at the Mall of America and found the people really friendly and helpful.

I had a go at snowboarding for the first time and even tho i only managed a small slope, i had my eye on the big ones - someday.

Like always, even tho i had a great time (jet lag aside 😄☐), its always great to come home. If the welcome that i got off my dog, Elvis is anything to go by , 2017 could be a great year. All i can say is ; bring it on !

Finally, a quote to finish
" no one now dies of fatal truths ; there are too many antidotes to them " --- Neitzsche.

Rònàn Faherty

December 14, 2016 ·

ARAN ISLANDS

My Christmas wish to You.

Good Evening,

My original thoughts were to write about my upcoming christmas holiday trip to America , primarily to see my brother, Rory and his family but i honestly feel compelled from my heart to mention breifly how writing this blog has changed my life for the better and to offer my heartfelt thanks to each and every one of you.

It is not a secret that i have an obvious disability and while on the one hand there is a very long list of things that i can not do and in truth this can be hard to accept some days.

The flip side of that is ; there is a massive list of things that i can do and that i love. Right at the very top of that list is writing out my thoughts and feelings in this blog.

I could never express my gratitude adequately to you all - but please know, your support and readership has had an incredibly positive and happy impact on my quality of life.

I now find myself really looking forward to next year.

Here's to many more future blogs from my Island Home.

Finally - i would sincerely like to wish you all a very Happy and Healthy Christmas.

Rònàn Faherty.

December 7, 2016 ·

ARAN ISLANDS

What I'll miss about home when i go away for Christmas.

Good Evening ,

I am sitting here and I'm thinking initially about what i will miss about my island home, but before i write on those bits that are close to my heart, a form of pattern has evolved over the last few years ;

I have finished working up at Dùn Aonghusa at the end of the summer and before i started writing this blog - which has changed my life --- i used to have a bleak period between the end of summer and going away for Christmas but while my job situation hasnt improved , my quality of life has , as a result of writing these few words on a weeklybasis, it has brought so much unexpected joy and happiness into my life.

I will very much miss Irish food as i find it to be the tastiest ive ever had - in other places, the food often looks brilliant but it can often lack taste.

The truth is ; you would stand in your bare feet in the snow to eat one of my mother's home cooked dinners.

I could write forever about the seas , the views, the fields , the cliffs , my neighbours --- the list is honestly endless but i really would like to mention how much i'll miss my dog , Elvis. Who is more than a pet - he is a companion and most of all , a friend.

At this stage , I would sincerely like to address those people who may have a disability - i would like to give them the biggest shout of encouragement and support that I can and kindly say ; if i can do it , so can you.

I'll finish with a quote of my own
" always belief in yourself - because if you dont -- who will ".

Rònàn Faherty.

November 30, 2016 ·

ARAN ISLANDS

Island Thoughts,

Good Evening,

This must be one of the most beautiful, still & calm nights that ive ever seen.

I am thinking alot about my upcoming trip to America to see my brother , Rory and his family for Christmas.

I have a lot of thoughts both about what i am looking forward to and what i'll miss about my island home when i go.
I would really like to write about these over the next couple of weeks before i go.

Right at this moment as i type my mind is very much taken with the fact that the ferry service to this island is stopping this evening until next march.

While i am certain that i may not know all the facts, i feel i would like to say that they ran an excellent service for 30 years and it will be greatly missed.

The loss of the daily ferry service is a huge loss to this island community and will impact negatively in all sorts of ways.

I'll finish with a quote
" youth is the gift of nature, but age is a work of art " --- Stanislaw Lee.

Rònàn Faherty.

November 23, 2016 ·

ARAN ISLANDS

An Unexpected but very Welcome burst of Beautiful Weather on my Island.

Good Evening,

This current spell of lovely weather is having such a positive and uplifting effect on my life - i find myself very tempted and leaning towards writing about being out in this glorious weather , going for walks and describing everything i see ---

But, the greatest impact and to be honest, the hardest one to write about, describe and articulate is the huge and incredibly positive impact this bright, crisp, clear weather has on my spirits.

I feel filled with positivity and looking out at this weather, i truly feel ;
Anything is Possible.

Thanks for reading.

Rònàn Faherty.

November 8, 2016 ·

ARAN ISLANDS

THOUGHTS , VIEWS, FEARS & HOPES FOR WINTER

Good Evening ,

I worked up at Dùn Aonghusa during the summertime and i expressed before how it made me feel very positive on a number of different levels.

As we head into winter i am faced with a huge variety of thoughts, hopes and to be honest, fears about this time of year.

Due to my disability, there are certain types of work that i just could not do - but, living with a disability has facilitated and always encouraged me to acknowledge what i cant do, but put my focus and energy towards what i can do.

My Father's people were fishermen and my Mother's people were farmers --- on the face of it, i can honestly do neither one, despite them being in my heart.

My Mother's people - the Concannons - were great innovators and entrepreneurs and my Father's people the Faherty's were self employed hunter gatheters at the sea ---
Now, not unlike most people - whether they have a disability or not - i can chose to lie down or draw on those wonderful positives

from the giants who's shoulders i stand on. That is my chosen route.

I am struggling to find a way, but i know in my heart that i will.

A Quote ;

" everyone has a disability, in some its more visible than in others ".

Thanks for reading.

Rònàn Faherty

October 31, 2016 ·

ARAN ISLANDS

POEM.

Good Evening,

I very much hope that you like my poem - i often stand outside my house and look in wonder up at the stars.
While i am gazing at them , i am aware that my view is both special and clear as there are no street lights or anyother competing lights where i live.

As i look up towards the Heavens at the Cosmos , i am humbled and always feel
grateful to see them from this beautiful Island.

While i am staring at the night sky and the twinkling stars , my thoughts go towards a life beyond our planet and i wonder ......

Thank you for reading.

Rònàn Faherty.

OUTER SPACE.

I look up from earth and try to see the planets
looking back at me, as we gase at bright gusty
stars they gase back at us.

We squint at the Milky Way, way up high and
look for Mars in the sky, where Neptune, Saturn,
Jupiter are gone, lost in empty of space.

Out in the vast never ending palace beyond our
home is the universe an unlimited place from
earth, together the stars shares it's life with the
living.

Twinkling little stars way up in the sky at night
as the sandy place of our moon sends some light
to our world, it gives hope to some creatures
that go in for search of food.

By Ronan Faherty.

October 12, 2016 ·

ARAN ISLANDS.

Memories of Pòrt Chorrùch,

Good Evening,

I am very fortunate to live on an island that has many beautiful and unspoilt places.

I could honestly write page after page about each and every one of them, but for now , with your kindness and understanding, id like to write from a completely personal point of view about a place that i really love called ; Loch Phòrt Chorrùch.

Its an unspoiled and completely natural lake that is beside the sea but it is freshwater and home to lots of wildlife , including ; otters, wild ducks, swans, herons and many many more.

I used to cycle a 3 wheeled bicycle as a result of my accident and being able to cycle to this simple but powerful place of beauty allowed me to sit and witness this beauty in it's most natural form and as many would believe , as God intended it to be.

Another huge part of this outing for me was, that my dear 3 wheeler bike gave me the independence to go there under my own steam - i don't want to labour this point but a sense of independence for someone who often relies on others is deeply satisfying, refreshing and the sense of wellbeing is practically indescribable.

I associate my time sitting in this natural place of beauty with my own small sense of achievment in cycling there.

Im aware that many people who arrive on this island off the ferries, jump onto bikes and cycle west and dont really give it a thought - i am truly happy for them.

I celebrate and take great pleasure in seeing them enjoy my home island.

Righly or wrongly, i sometimes think ;
You never miss the water, until the well runs dry.

Rònàn Faherty.

September 28, 2016 ·
ARAN ISLANDS.

My Brother Rory's return.

Good Evening,

My Brother Rory lives in minnesota, and last week, himself and his wife, Kari were home for a wedding.
It was a very happy ocassion for my family - myself included - but a massive highlight for me was Rory's return.
I cant be 100 % sure if this is the correct forum or not but either way, id like to very briefly express some of my feelings about my big brother Rory.

I would only being telling the truth in saying that, Rory was and is my hero.
Since we were kids , i always felt safe and secure in the knowledge that Rory always kept and eye out for me - most especially because of my accident but more importantly and vitally, because he is my loving big brother.

I always look forward to seeing him , more than i am adequately able express - it warms my heart.

I will finish with a quote
" when you build bridges, you can keep crossing them "

Rònàn Faherty.

September 13, 2016 ·

ARAN ISLANDS

Summer and work finishes - new challenges ahead.

Good Evening,

There are many many changes ocurring as we head into autumn and towards winter.

I will write in more detail about nature's fascinating and glorious changes but for now id just like to lightly touch on the personal dilemma that the end of the summer brings to my life ;

Each summer, i have been lucky enough to work up at Dun Aonghusa and while having a sense of purpose gave a great structure and by extension , it enhanced my sense of self and thus my quality of life - one of the main benefits and pluses was ;

meeting people from all different walks of life. I found this very interesting.

Aside from dealing with the downsides to not working , i will miss greatly meeting the people who visited my home island and who were so interested in it and appreciative of it.

Until next year - thank you so much and i am already looking forward to next year.

Rònàn Faherty.

August 30, 2016 ·

ARAN ISLANDS.

DUN EOGHNACHTA, INIS MOR.

Good Evening,

I find this a strange thing to express but even though dun eoghnachta is up behind my house and very close to my heart, this is only my third ever time going up there.

As i mentioned before - my walk is not brilliant and the walk up there is one that i find quite difficult.

If it wasnt for this blog post, im certain that i wouldnt have done it this summer at all - so , along with thanking each and every reader for giving me the boost , i would like to express my gratitude to my mother , Agnes for her company and assistance --- i would also like give a shout out to my dog , Elvis for coming too.

I feel great at having gone up there and it has shown me ; looking at it through my back window is one thing but actually going up there, really is another thing altogether.

I hope you enjoy the video.

Ill finish with a quote of my own
" work hard, dream big - and your dreams might come true "

Rònàn Faherty.

August 23, 2016 ·

ARAN ISLANDS.

The Uphill Walk Behind My House.

Good Evening,

The walk up behind my house goes towards Dun Eoghnachta - it's a very challenging and strenuous hill to go up , to be honest i find it especially difficult
as my walk is not brilliant.
For every footstep and every bead of sweat , you are rewarded with a view that could only melt your heart while taking your breath away - in every sense.
I was accompanied on my walk by my Mother , Agnes - my aunt , Angela and of course , not forgetting my faithful dog and friend ; Elvis.

I hope you enjoy my home views as much as ive enjoyed sharing them with you. The beautiful and ancient fort of Dun Eoghnachta is a place that is very close to my heart and i would dearly love to share some of my thoughts with you about this magical , spiritual and celtic place - going forward.

Id like to finish this week with a quote that i read

" life is wasted on the living "

--- by Douglas Noel Adams.

Rònàn Faherty.

August 2, 2016 ·

ARAN ISLANDS.

Change.

Good Evening ,

This island, for a whole lot of reasons, encourages reflection and if i were to leave it there it would be a very fair and valid point.

The Island has been responsible for bringing a multitude of changes into thousands of people's lives.

Sometimes the changes are in the form of a memorable and stand out day or few days but i have seen first hand, the island magic impact positively and change people's lives for the better forever.

I had a burning desire to move back to my home Island - where i was born, my parents , grandparents and all belonging to me were born and reared.
The desire to come took alot of effort , action and dedication but every bit has been worthwhile.

This period of my life and this topic is deeply personal and important to me and i would very much like to expand on this again sometime.

Finally, a quote of my own

"Age is only a number and there is no such thing as old age "

Rònàn Faherty.

July 26, 2016 ·

ARAN ISLANDS.

The " Swallows " Return to their home Island.

Good Evening,

For many years on this island , as the building sites in places like ;
London,
Birmingham & South Boston shut down for their summer holidays - the hardy souls, digging the trenches and mixing the concrete came back to their home island where they were born and reared but sadly had to leave.

These fine men and women returned, like clockwork at the beging of august every year --- their return not only brought inexpressible joy to their families but to our community too.

Their love and connection can be loosly written as ; they may have left the island , but the island never leaves them. Even though this says alot, in truth, it barely scratches the surface in describing the deep and , at times, savage love they had in their hearts for their home island.

The patterns, frequency & ease of the homecomings has changed , somewhat, but the depth of the emotions, ties and connections remains as strong as ever it was.

Having lived on the mainland for a number of years, my identification with the " returning swallows " , runs deep and i not only see their joy but i feel it too.

Failte aras mo chairde.

Rònàn Faherty.

July 12, 2016 ·

ARAN ISLANDS

Noble men of the past exchange goods and show us the way.

Good Evening ,

When i was sitting at the harbour watching the old style sailing boats - hookers - coming in from Connemara , i thought back to my parents, grand parents and great grand parents time when the hard working and teak tough , turf men of connemara sent out their precious and highly valued turf with the connemara boatmen who knew no fear but had a respect, love and knowledge of the sea - that came down through many generations and was in their blood and was their way of life.

These noble and true men, brought turf to the men of Aran, who had no bogland but for generations had fearlessly harvested the sea and therefore had fish to barter for turf.

In most cases, no money changed hands and while we have alot of terminology today ; food miles, carbon footprint , slow food etc etc --- these fine men had no such terminology but respectfully bartered with eachother to fulfill needs on both sides. Everyone was a winner and all today's very valid terminology was covered with a bit to spare.

In looking at how the these fine and true men conducted their business , i believe we can learn some simple yet powerful lessons.

I would very much like to finish with a quote of my own if i may
" those who dont know great citizens are destined to be great people "

Rònàn Faherty.

July 5, 2016 ·

ARAN ISLANDS.

Island thoughts.

Good Evening,

There is a wonderful and unexpected magic that happens every single time that i take a walk on my island home.

It usually takes the form of awakening thoughts that have been gently prompted and coaxed out by encountering nature and the elements.

When i saw the two seagull chicks in the first picture , on the cliff edge - i thought about the times that i attempted something for the first time - whether it was a first day at school , a first day at work , a first date , a swim on a cold day --- to be honest, the list could go

on forever but two things really stand out ;
I always felt nervous and aprehensive
AND
Im always always glad i did it afterwards.

I left the cliffs thinking about my little feathered friends and felt a strange but real solidarity with them as they faced their first flight.

Finally , a quote
" justice delayed, is justice denied"
William Gladstone.

Rònàn Faherty.

June 21, 2016 ·

ARAN ISLANDS

ISLAND SUNSETS

Good Evening,

I live at the Western end of this Island and many people, before me, have said that it is the most beautiful place in Western Europe - i would find it impossible to argue with that.

Sunsets are an important and valued part of life back here in the West. They are a feature in our daily lives.

When i have been away from my Island home, one of the treasures i carry is the view of the setting sun in my mind's eye. I carry so many images of home in my heart and right up there is the sun setting in the west.

I feel very connected and in touch with home when i see a sunset - it fills my heart and always produces a longing for home that comes from a very tender and deep place.

Instead of finishing with a quote - this week --- i hope my picture of myself will help people to connect with me, my island , my thoughts and my poems.

Rònàn Faherty.

June 14, 2016 ·

ARAN ISLANDS

My Grandfather - Tommy Faherty.

Good Evening,

I wrote some time ago about my 4 grandparents - all , sadly passed away - and the wonderfully positive and everlasting impact that they have had and , indeed, continue to have on my life.

It was with enormous pleasure that i stumbled across the picture of my Grandfather , Tommy Faherty , in a posting by the Naomh Eanna Trust .
It was really heartwarming to see this shot as i didnt have any picture of him - only my own memories.

This was a look back and a snap shot of island life and the signifance of the steamer that was our link with the outside world.

I also put up a picture of my own father , Bertie Faherty and along with my grandparents and my mother , Agnes , id really love to write a little more about them and the irreplacable part they have played in my life and i hope to do some justice to them in expressing my gratitude and love to them while attempting to show them the place they have in my heart. The treasured and often unexpressed memories of my heart.

Finally, for this week , a quote of my own
" some of us dream of success while others, work for it ".

 Rònàn Faherty.

June 7, 2016 ·

ARAN ISLANDS.

Summer work on my Island home.

Good Afternoon,

The pictures below are representative of summer on my Island home.
Another summer change that has occured over the last 5 years or so is ; i have been fortunate to have been working up at The ancient and stunningly beautiful fort of Dun Aonghusa.

The reality of those scenes from the photos are that they really uplift and invigourate my daily life but very importantly to me - going to work gives me a great sense of purpose each day and is a huge boost to my own sense of dignity and self respect.
Very often in the winter when i have no work , my days can drift if i allow them.

My job is providing more than money and it means alot to me.

I will finish with a quote
" brevity is the soul of lingerie "
Dorothy Parker.

Rònàn Faherty.

May 31, 2016 ·
ARAN ISLANDS

MY POEM THAT CAME FROM MY HEART AND MY BEAUTIFUL ISLAND HOME.

Good Evening,

The poem that is truly my gift to you, took me 5 weeks to write - it stopped and started and stopped and started many times.
The only answer i had was to go out in the elements and go into Mother Nature and to trust that process.
Mother Nature freed my mind and somehow allowed me find the words that were eluding and avoiding my mind.
Im not 100% sure if i was trying too hard or not but i feel happy to let this poem out to you dear readers and feel that if ever a place influenced and drove a poem - this is it.
Thank you Aran and thank you readers.

If i could i would sincerly like to thank my sister Cliodhna Faherty for her kind permission in using the first photo.

Id like if possible to finish with a quote
of my own
" i can accept not winning but cannot accept not trying "

Ronan Faherty.

LEGENDS NEVER DEPART.

True iconic singers furthermore actors and actress of the silver screen never pass on, they live forever in the public eye, from then and now to the end of time, they will stay in the public view and will always exist.

They are all well-known famous individuals of our golden years, with our days gone will be remembered for a lifetime, when melodies sounds, gone is the earth we know, her flowers in vision.

Sprit of yesterdays music is gone and will never beforegotten and all the others too, days of grief are days of grace, remember that it's love that is Impossible to bear, yet music is what they share.

And far into the night he crooned that tune, as singer stopped playing and went to bed, while the weary blues echoed through his head, a piano is trying to break a molecule, around the red spotlights.

Beautiful melodies and tunes of today and yesterday will live forever, the chippies talk about the funnies in the papers, we often remember the lyrics to our favorite songs, and we get excited whenever we hear them on the radio or on our mp3 players.

By Ronan Faherty.

May 24, 2016 ·

ARAN ISLANDS

Island Thoughts.

Good Evening,

I wanted very much to have a poem written this evening but the more i seemed to force it , the further it got away from me.

The only way that i know how to free my mind and embrace this process is to go out and walk in the fresh air.

I walk the shoreline , the roads and the cliffs of my island home and find that even though its not that easy to write poetry on demand - i am totally inspired by my home island and filled with a deep sense of gratitude for living in my homeplace.

I hope to write a little more of my poem this week , as like my home place - my poems fill my heart.

Id really like to finish with a quote
" one day , in retrospect, the years of struggle will strike you as the most beautiful "
Sigmund Freud.

Ronan Faherty.

May 17, 2016 ·

ARAN ISLANDS

The expected and the unexpected on my Island Summer walk.

Good Evening ,

Last Saturday i hit off from home with two specific destinations in mind but as so very often happens out here to me , it was item 3 that i hadnt planned that has had the most lasting and indeed , profound effect on me.

Firstly , i was aware that a helicopter was dropping off building materials at the ancient fort of Dun Aonghusa - as i watched with admiration as the pilot bravely manouvered his flying machine , i found my thoughts rolling back to the early inhabitants of this spectacular fort and i wondered , in their wildest dreams could the noble folk of the Fir Bolg ever have imagined such circumstances as a helicopter dropping off materials to their home. It allowed me ponder how futile looking into and stressing about the future actually is --- the truth is ; we just dont know but will know when we need to.

With these thoughts carrying me , i set off to see the vintage car rally at the local hotel. I am full of admiration for the people who restore and maintain these beautiful machines. I recognise a labour of love when i see it and whether its cars , boats or old buildings the one common denomenator is a genuine love of the subject. When i got to the hotel to view these machines , i certainly was not disappointed and found it thrilling to see these fully and lovingly restored machines that are so well maintained.
On my way to the Hotel , i passed by a house in the village of Kilronan , called St Ronans --- i have passed this house many times but on Saturday morning for no reason that i can logically explain , i found myself deeply impacted by my connection to this house as my Grandfather , Eamon Concannon was born there.
It brought some unexpected but treasured memories of my daideo and im aware that i have written briefly about my relationship with him before - i feel that , with your permission, that id love to share more on this some time in the future.

Thank you for reading and id like to finish with a quote
" Absence of proof is not proof of Absence "
Michael Critchon.

Ronan Faherty.

January 20, 2016 ·

ARAN ISLANDS

Fond memories of an early boat trip home.

Good Morning,

Hello everyone - my name is Rónán Faherty and I very much look forward to sharing some of my thoughts with you.

My first conscious memory of taking the boat home, was on a steamer called ; The Naomh Eanna.

A number of memories stand out for me - the discussion, all in irish, on the boat about whether she'd go to the islands first or straight home to Arainn.
Also, the sense that a trip to Galway was a special event unlike the every day occurrence it is now.

Watching the cargo deliveries at the islands while the Naomh Eanna was at anchor and watching the skill and courage of the currach men was a sight that I feel privileged to have seen and I know it's likes won't be seen again.

I can't really explain it logically but the Taytos, Chocolate and Red Lemonade tasted so much better aboard the boat.

The first sighting of my home island of Inis Mor always brought a unique, exciting and warm feeling --- a set of feelings that has always been reserved for my island homecomings.

I will try and keep writing each week and I hope that you enjoy them as I certainly have enjoyed writing this.

Lastly, I would like to end with a quote ---

This week its from Charlotte Bronte.

"A ruffled mind, makes a restless pillow "

Rónán Faherty.

May 9, 2016 ·

ARAN ISLANDS

ISLAND INSPIRATIONS

Good Evening,

I took these photos myself when i was out and about and each one brought up different thoughts and feelings and id really like to share some them with you all this evening.

The Factory - to me it represents a new way of working to the life we have always known. Even though its not run as a factory today - the land was donated by my grandfather , who like many at the time , were very happy to see people having the choice stay at home and be a part of our community. 3 of my aunts worked there ; Delia , Catherine & Anne.
It was very positive in our community.

The Church (onaght) --- religion has been massively important in my community to date but how important it will be in the next generation remains to be seen. Our community needs to be financially viable firstly while looking to the future , all the time embracing , honouring and integrating our rich past.

The currach and the blacksmith --- i feel it in a very deep way that fishing will always be in our blood. Its our island way of life.

7 Churches --- historically this was a university and significantly , education is the overwhelming choice of the next generation, they reasonably chose this over tailing prawns on the deck of a boat or tending to a small and uneconomical holding.

Summary - id like to develop and share my thoughts on these topics further at a later date but for now, a thought that keeps coming to me as i write is " theres more to life than money".

Ill finish with a quote of my own --- " life is hard , but if youre going to live it - youve got to be tough ".

Ronan Faherty.

May 5, 2016 ·

ARAN ISLANDS

A Poem Inspired by my travels

Good Evening ,

I hope you like my poem - it comes straight from my heart.

I wrote this poem sitting in the small room in the back of the house but it was very much inspired by my travels --- when i was going over to America with my mother to visit my brother, Rory , i got a clear view of my home island from up above.

I always feel full of joy when i travel and actually humbled. My thoughts are exciting and a big part of me feels that i am leaving my troubles behind me.

This is escapism to a point but part of me always knows that i must return to reality and all that entails.

The poems i write are very personal and come from a special and tender place within me and even though i sometimes experience a shyness or reluctance in putting them out there - i am so so grateful for all the people that read them and it brings huge joy and happiness into my life.

Finally, a quote

" how often misused words generate misleading thoughts "
Herbert Spencer.

Ronan Faherty.

April 26, 2016 ·

ARAN ISLANDS

Island Inspiration

Good Afternoon,

I am working on writing a poem of my own and had initially
hoped that it might be ready for today.

I know some people can just sit at a desk and write but for me, it
kinda works differently.
I draw alot of inspiration from where I live and find when I go out
for a walk and feel the Atlantic breeze in my face and hear the roar
of the ocean, I very often come home inspired and ready to write.
These days I sometimes bring a notebook with me to try and
capture my thoughts as they come in , with Mother Nature's
assistance.

163

I will do my very best to have my poem ready for next week and I thank you all , sincerely , for your continued support.
I'm grateful.

Quote ---
"Rich gifts wax poor when givers prove unkind "
William Shakespeare.

Rónán Faherty.

April 19, 2016 ·

ARAN ISLANDS,

Personal memories of the Concannon Vineyard.

Good Evening,

I mentioned last week about the joy that I have experienced by revisiting my personal and childhood memories through these pages.
The effects have been extremely positive and I have thoroughly enjoyed my travels back through my family history.

My mother, Agnes is a Concannon and I clearly remember as a child hearing all about the Concannon Vineyard in California and as a family we've always taken a keen interest in it.

I would love to visit it
someday and have heard wonderful stories about it from my Uncle Mairtin
(Mairtin Eamonn) , who was fortunate enough to visit it some years ago.

The people who started the vineyard are my relatives and they left this island primarily for economic reasons - survival - but it would do them a great diservice not to mention their adventurous and pioneering spirit.

With this island spirit of innovation and independence, it's no surprise that this vineyard is the oldest ongoing winery in America.

The details and information
about the Concannon Vineyard are available online but, if I may,
I'd really like to express what it means from a personal and family
point of view.

These relatives of mine, that I never knew personally- left this
impossibly beautiful but barren island with no more than the
clothes on their backs.
They went by boat to America and whatever they may have lacked
in material possessions, they more than made up for with their
dreams, ambitions, independent minds and thirst for adventure.
In my own humble way, I'd like to pay these people both past and
present , the highest tribute that I possibly can.

I feel deeply honoured to have this family connection and would
like to thank you all for the chance to express this here.

I'm currently working on a poem and hope to have it ready for
next week or the week after but in the meantime, I'll finish with a
quote ---
"A certain amount of danger is essential to the quality of life ".
Charles Lindberg.

Rónán Faherty.

April 12, 2016 ·

ARAN ISLANDS

Family Memories of a daring escape.

Good Evening,

One of the effects of going down memory lane or , botharin na
Smaointe - in my native tongue, is that it has opened up a store of
treasured memories that were buried and seemingly forgotten.
I have also found that I have fortunately managed to access my
own family history and the other day , inspired by these events -
my mother, Agnes and my uncle Mairtin told me a story from long
ago that touched my heart and impacted on me very positively.

165

At the begining of the war of independence, the black and tans came to this island looking for rebels. My great grandfather Tomas Fleming was married to Liam O Flaherty 's sister - who's name was Agnes just like my own mother.

The local police had to accompany the black and tans to the small cottage in the village of Gort na gCapaill where my great grandfather was living.

The police only showed the black and tans the windows on the eastern gable and "omitted" to let the black and tans know that there was also a window on the western gable that the brave Tomas escaped through.

He made his way by ;

Port Bheal an Duin , Poll na bpeist, Dun Aonghusa and eventually to a safe house where he found the warmest of aran welcomes.

I was filled with a strong and almost overwhelming sense of pride and admiration for his bravery that was only driven by his heartfelt belief in irish freedom and fairness for all.

A selfless act that is rare in today's world.

I'd like to finish with a quote of my own if I could ---

" tunes , melodies & harmonies are my poetry and music of days gone by "

Rónán Faherty.

January 19, 2016 ·

ARAN ISLANDS

CHANGE

Good Morning,

Another stunning Island morning - great to be alive.

For the forseeable future, I will be collaborating and posting with a neighbour and friend called, Rónán Faherty.

Rónán will post once a week and I am asking and appealing to the readers who have been so kind to me and supportive of me - to please give Rónán the same chance, opportunity and level of support.

Rónán is a very true son of this rugged and beautiful island. His father and his father's family were and are men of the sea. It would not be stretching it to say that salt water flows through their veins. These noble people have an unrivalled knowledge, love and instinct for all matters maritime and if you ever found yourself in rough conditions - it's one of them you'd want beside you.
Brave Aran Fishermen.

Rónán ' s mother's family are equally distinguished and noble people.
While Rónán ' s grandfather and all belonging to them worked , understood and loved the land - this is only a tiny part of their wonderful story.
The Concannons were and are ; entrepreneurs, innovators, thinkers and doers.
Rónán s grandmother taught many children here over the years and there's many a person that can honestly say they owe her a massive debt of gratitude for the caring way in which she imparted knowledge and a love of learning.
Rónán s grandmother also was a neice of the great Island writer , Liam O Flaherty ---

In short, Rónán has the truest island experiences to share and once again I am asking that you please give these short pieces that will follow a fair chance.

Thank you.

Conor Meehan.

That is a selection from the blogs that I have written and I hope that you have enjoyed them – those blogs proved to be the catalyst in bringing about some very significant changes in my life. I have always secretly wanted to write and to be honest, I just wasn't sure how to go about it or indeed, if anyone would be interested in what I had to say.

I mentioned before that I am very driven by the fact that my story may end up helping, inspiring or encouraging someone and it was this thought that really got me out of my comfort zone. I certainly don't want to put myself up there as an example of anything and am as full of human fears and doubts as the next person, but I think it's probably fair to say that I have a hard hand of cards to play and even though the first and initial thoughts can be negative, frightening and nearly cause you to give up – if I have anything of value to say, please let me say this as clearly and strongly as I possibly can - DON'T GIVE UP.

There is always hope and there are always ways to work with what you have. I am asking every single human being that reads my story – which in reality was harder on my family than myself - to keep on keeping on.

We are not seeking perfection but are, earnestly chasing progress.

I will sign off on my story now and only wish to say one last thing:

Thank You!

Printed in Poland
by Amazon Fulfillment
Poland Sp. z o.o., Wrocław

48998589R00100